THE COMPLETE OUTDOORSMAN'S GUIDE TO

EDIBLE WILD PLANTS

THE COMPLETE OUTDOORSMAN'S GUIDE TO

EDIBLE WILD PLANTS

BERNDT BERGLUND & CLARE E. BOLSBY

CHARLES SCRIBNER'S SONS
NEW YORK

Illustrated by E. B. Sanders

LC 77-82243
ISBN 0-684-15480-3 *case*
     0-684-15481-1 *paper*
Printed and bound in the United States

To Clare and Santon Bolsby,
who have in so many ways helped to make
this project possible

Contents

Foreword

This book contains fifty wild plants to have fun with. Its purpose is to chronicle the facts about some of the wild vegetables and fruits indigenous to North America and to suggest methods by which these foods may be prepared and served.

We have concentrated on recipes that have particular value for demonstrating simple culinary principles used by the early settlers of this continent. This tradition, taste, technical skill, and respect for ingredients is the basis for good cooking everywhere.

It is to the beginner as well as the advanced cook that this book is dedicated. But whether novice or expert, we would like to emphasize the need to follow these recipes precisely, especially the first few times you make them. Improvisation and experimentation are essential ingredients in imaginative cooking and yet, if you consider that most of these dishes were refined by our early settlers — cooks who undoubtedly experienced many failures before success — then you are less likely, initially, to want to diverge from them.

For the more experienced outdoor cook, we hope that some of the unfamiliar recipes which follow will be fresh discoveries and that our detailed descriptions will contain an insight or two of value. And to the beginner, we would like to point out that these recipes explore only a small area of the complex territory of cooking wild plants.

We owe a great deal of respect and gratitude to the frontier women who spent many hours cooking under primitive conditions so as to have nutritious meals on the table and keep starvation at bay. We are thankful, too, that they had the foresight to record their successes so that we who follow might have the opportunity to seek out and enjoy the intriguing variety of edible plants in Mother Nature's pantry.

This book would have been impossible to write without help from many people. Our thanks go to these friends for their invaluable advice and encouragement.

Weights and measurements have had to be converted to modern-day terms and are as close as possible to the original recipes. We assure you that endless hours have been spent in the kitchen to test them.

Special thanks go to Frances MacIlquham for advice and suggestions which have undoubtedly improved this book. Also to our friend, Bev Sanders, for countless hours spent at his drawing board to produce these delightful drawings. Without them this book would not be complete.

Preparing Wild Plants 1

Many cooks destroy the nutrients in greens and vegetables by over-cooking. Remember that to preserve vital minerals and vitamins, particularly Vitamin C, over-cooking should be avoided.

Ideally, concern with nutritional values should not lead us to overlook how delicious these vegetables are. Times given in our recipes are average cooking times but should be adjusted according to the freshness of the vegetable. Unfortunately, if you want to enjoy seasonal wild roots or tubers all year round, you have to make the best of vegetables that have been stored for some time. We know how impractical it is for the city dweller to keep fresh vegetables in an old fashioned root cellar but storage problems can often be overcome with proper care. If stored in small amounts, vegetables are less prone to deterioration from rot and mildew.

In fact, cooking vegetables is a simple affair and a matter of timing more than anything else. There are two basic methods. All wild leaves should be covered and steamed with the minimum amount of water. Wild roots or tubers, on the other hand, are cooked uncovered in plenty of boiling water, drained, and served as soon as possible.

Never put roots and tubers in cold water for cooking — bring the water to a rolling boil first. Cooked in this fashion, root vegetables preserve their color, freshness, and flavor to a remarkable degree. But if not served at once, they will taste as though they have been subjected to a restaurant warming oven.

A wise precaution is to cook all vegetables in enamel, oven-proof glass, or stainless steel pans and dishes. Many roots and tubers absorb a metallic taste from aluminum or iron pans and some tend to discolor badly. Braising is a good way to prepare fresh vegetables because they are half steamed in a little stock and butter. The cooking liquid, when reduced, can be used as a sauce. Although not the simplest method, braising will preserve nutrients and flavor. Since the vegetables are cooked rather slowly over-cooking can be avoided and, if necessary, may be kept warm for a reasonable length of time without losing any of their delicate flavor. Cooking juices are excellent for gravies and sauces as they contain the vitamins and minerals.

To make a green salad, shredding a few green leaves and pouring some dressing over them does not sound complicated. But to the French, it is a precise affair indeed. This applies to salad making with wild greens too.

The plain green salad may be simple to prepare but because of its very simplicity it can be exceedingly dull unless made with the utmost care. A green salad is only as good as the greens that are in it. When selecting the ingredients, include only the choicest fresh greens, remove all tinted or wilted leaves, and tear the leaves, rather than using a knife. If you plan to serve more than one green, the choice is important. It's far better to limit yourself to only two or three greens of contrasting flavor and texture. For example, in the fall, when dandelion leaves are rather bitter, combine them with watercress to emphasize the bitter-sweet taste.

Whatever greens you choose, try to make your salad as soon as possible after they are picked. Wash them thoroughly under cold running water, shake off the excess and gently pat dry with paper towels. The importance of bone dry greens cannot be stressed too strongly. Moisture will spoil the dressing and, ultimately, the salad.

Whenever you serve a salad, make sure that the ingredients and the salad bowl itself are chilled. Salad should not be served in a wooden bowl because wood is a poor conductor of heat and cold. You may like to impress family or guests and toss the salad at the table at the last minute. Instead, do it in the kitchen. Here you can roll up your sleeves and use your hands. Not only will the salad be more thoroughly mixed but you are less likely to bruise the tender greens. And of course, before serving, taste the salad for seasoning. We have found that we always undersalt greens and it's surprising how a little bit of extra salt will enhance the flavor.

When you are collecting edible wild plants, you should take into consideration that most people regard these plants as weeds. If gathered near farms, along roadsides, or even in some gardens, you have to be sure that the plants have not been sprayed with weed killer. And so it's preferable to forage for healthy specimens in undisturbed areas where there is less chance that they have been in contact with dangerous chemicals.

A vital point to remember is to positively identify the plants you pick. Many plants look alike yet one may be edible and the other slightly poisonous.

Wild plants are not only fun to collect, they are also fun to cook, as we shall discover in the following pages.

Edible Nuts

2

ROCKY MOUNTAIN NUT PINE *(Pinus edulis)*

This small pine tree is found from Colorado south and west into Mexico, and in great numbers in New Mexico. Usually the trunk is short but it can reach a height of thirty feet. The short, stiff leaves are an inch long and grouped in pairs. The fruits or cones are often wider than they are long and are light brown, glossy, and thickly scaled. The seeds are about half an inch long and slightly flattened.

The seeds were used in great quantities by the Indians and Mexicans, who utilized the packrat to gather them. Tearing the nest apart, they could find as much as a pound of seeds in one nest. The seeds were an important article of trade for the Indians in southern California, where the nuts from the One Leaved Nut Pine *(Pinus monopylla)* are gathered in great quantities.

Often taking the place of wheat for the Indians in the southwestern mountains, nuts were gathered late in the fall before the snows, and eaten raw or roasted. To produce flour, the nuts were ground between two stones; or a coarse gruel was made, the water allowed to evaporate, and the remainder sieved and stored for winter use.

PIÑON NUT HARD TACK

2 cups white flour	1 teaspoon salt
2 cups piñon nut flour	warm water
2 tablespoons shortening	

Sift the flours together so that they are well mixed. Add the shortening, salt, and enough warm water to make a soft dough which will handle easily. Roll out into very thin cakes about 6 inches in diameter. Cook in a heavy cast iron pan or on top of a wood stove. If in the bush, bake on a heated flat rock. Allow to dry in the oven or close to the fire.

PIÑON NUT FLOUR CREAM PORRIDGE

2 cups sour cream   1 cup piñon nut flour

Place the sour cream in a 2-quart saucepan, and bring to the boil. Stirring constantly, add enough flour to make a medium thick mush or, even better, use an egg beater. As the fat rises to the surface, pour it off and save. Keep stirring until more fat rises, then add more flour to make a thick gruel.

Add scalded milk until of the desired consistency. Serve with butter and cold milk.

PIÑON NUT FLOUR TORTILLAS

2 ¼ cups piñon nut flour   1¹/₃ cups cold water
1 teaspoon salt

Preheat the oven to 250°F. In a mixing bowl, combine the flour and the salt; gradually pour in one cup of the cold water, stirring constantly. Knead the mixture with your hands, adding more water, a tablespoon at a time, until the dough becomes firm and no longer sticks to the fingers. Divide the dough into four batches and with a rolling pin roll out the dough between long strips of waxed paper until the dough is about 1x6 inch thick. With a lid as a guide and a sharp knife, cut out rounds about 5 inches in diameter. Stack the rounds between pieces of waxed paper.

Heat an 8-inch cast iron skillet over moderate heat. One by one, cook the tortillas for 2 minutes on each side, until golden brown. Keep warm in the oven until all the tortillas are made.

DEVILLED EGGS WITH PIÑON NUTS

6 hard-cooked eggs   ¹/₄ cup piñon nuts, crushed
¹/₄ teaspoon salt   2 tablespoons butter
¹/₂ teaspoon mustard   2 tablespoons cream

Cut the hard-cooked eggs in half lengthwise. Spoon out the yolks and place in a mixing bowl; add the salt, mustard, piñon nuts, butter, and cream. With a rotary beater or wire whisk, beat until well mixed and soft. Place the egg halves on a lettuce leaf. Put the yolk mixture in a cookie press fitted with a star nozzle, and fill the egg halves with the mixture. Garnish with sprigs of parsley.

Rocky Mountain Nut Pine

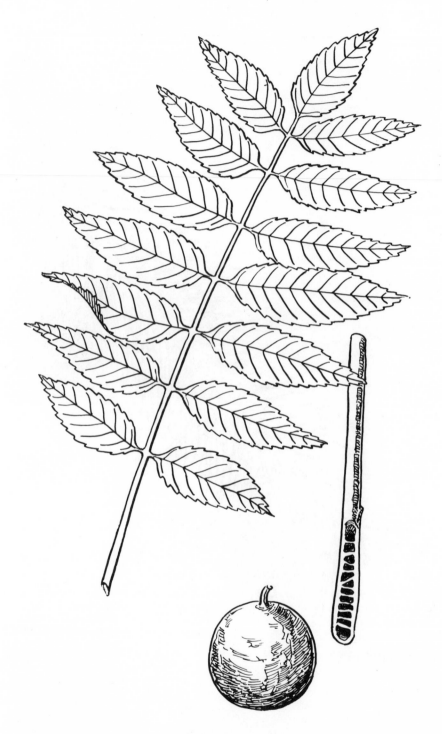

Black Walnut

BLACK WALNUT (*Juglans nigra*)

Unfortunately, this stately tree is on the decline, as indiscriminate felling for its valuable wood continues all over North America. Its natural habitat extends from eastern Canada and the United States, south to Florida and Texas, but it is rarely found in the West except in reforested areas. The black walnut is one of the most important of our native nut-bearing trees. Walnuts range in stature from small to large trees with a furrowed, scaly bark and large deciduous, alternate, aromatic, compound leaves. It has stout twigs with conspicuous leaf scars. The male flowers are borne in drooping catkins growing from lateral buds on the past season's growth. In contrast, the female flowers are borne in short, sparsely flowered spikes on the tips of the new growth. The fruit is a thick-shelled nut, and is enclosed in a semi-fleshy, more or less hairy husk. The nuts mature in the fall and drop soon after.

Usually the hardest part of dealing with these nuts is separating the husks from the shell. The early settlers and the Indians would spread the freshly gathered nuts in the sun until they were partly dried, when the husks were easily shucked off. Through this natural drying process, the nuts lost their inherent bitterness.

WALNUT BRITTLE

2 cups sugar
1 cup corn syrup
2 cups walnuts, chopped
¹/₂ cup water

1 tablespoon butter
1 teaspoon vanilla
2 teaspoons baking soda

In a large cast iron frying pan mix the sugar, corn syrup, and water. Cook over low heat until the mixture reaches the soft ball stage. (This can be tested by dropping a teaspoonful of the mixture into a cup of cold water; if it has the consistency you want, stop the cooking. If you like a hard brittle, continue cooking a little longer.) Remove from the heat, stir in the walnuts, and add butter, vanilla, and baking soda. Blend quickly and pour on to a well-greased cookie sheet. While slightly soft and still on the cookie sheet, score into squares with a sharp knife.

WALNUT CRUST COLD MAPLE SOUFFLE

1 tablespoon unflavored
  gelatin
¹/₄ cup cold water
1 cup maple syrup

2 eggs, separated
pinch of salt
1 pint whipping cream

Soften the gelatin in cold water. Beat the syrup and egg yolks together in the top half of a double boiler. Set the pan over the boiling water, heat, and stir for about five minutes. Remove the pan from the water; stir in the softened gelatin. When the gelatin has dissolved, chill the mixture in the refrigerator until the consistency of jam or honey — the mixture should not be too thick. Stir occasionally as it sets.

Beat the egg whites and salt until moist peaks form. Fold in the thickened maple mixture, then the stiffly whipped cream. Spoon the maple mixture into the walnut crust in a spring-form pan. Garnish with walnuts. Cover and chill for several hours or overnight.

Walnut Crust

1¹/₂ cups chopped walnuts
3 tablespoons brown sugar

3 tablespoons melted butter

Combine the ingredients. Press the mixture over the bottom of the spring-form pan. Bake in a 400°F oven for 6 to 7 minutes. Cool before filling with the chilled maple mixture.

EGG AND WALNUT SLICES IN SYRUP

2 teaspoons butter, softened
8 egg yolks
¹/₄ cup walnuts, pulverized in
  a blender or ground in a nut
  grinder

1 lemon
2 cups sugar
2 cups water
2 three-inch cinnamon
  sticks

Coat the sides and bottom of a 3-cup heat-proof mold with the softened butter. In a large mixing bowl, beat the egg yolks and walnuts together with a wire whisk, until the yolks are thick and pale yellow. Pour the mixture into the mold and cover tightly with a sheet of buttered aluminum foil. Place the mold in a deep pot. Fill with boiling water to just below the rim of the mold and bring back to a boil over high heat. Cover the pot, reduce the heat, and simmer for 25 minutes. Run the blade of a knife around the inside edge of the mold and turn out on to a plate.

With a sharp knife, remove the peel of the lemon, taking care that you don't get any of the bitter white pith with the peel. Cut the peel into half-inch strips. Combine the peel, sugar, water, and cinnamon sticks in a 2-quart saucepan. Bring to a boil over high heat, stirring constantly until the sugar dissolves. Boil briskly for about 5 minutes. Pour the mixture over the egg cake and chill in the refrigerator for at least 3 hours.

WALNUT CAKE

6 eggs, separated	$^3/_4$ cup sugar
1 whole egg	$^1/_3$ cup bread crumbs
1 cup ground walnuts	1 teaspoon flour

Preheat the oven to 275°F. In a large mixing bowl, beat the egg yolks and the whole egg together with a wire whisk. Beat until the mixture is thick and light yellow in color. Gradually beat in the half cup of sugar, then the ground walnuts and the bread crumbs. Beat until the mixture forms a dense, moist mass. In another bowl, beat the egg whites until they begin to foam, then add the quarter cup of sugar, one tablespoon at a time. Beat until the whites form stiff unwavering peaks when the beater is lifted from the bowl. Fold a quarter of the egg whites into the walnut mixture, then sprinkle with the flour and fold in the remainder of the egg whites.

Butter and flour a 10-inch spring-form pan, discard excess flour, and pour the batter into the form, smoothing the top with a spoon. Bake the cake in the middle of the oven for 40 minutes. Remove from the oven and allow to cool before you slice it into two equal layers. Fill the cake with whipped cream and garnish with chopped walnuts.

BUTTERNUT (*Juglans cinerea*)

The butternut tree is a small to medium-sized tree, seldom exceeding seventy feet in height or three feet in diameter. It grows farther north than the black walnut, extending through New Brunswick and Ontario, south to Georgia and Alabama, and west to Arkansas and the Dakotas.

The trunk is usually short and divided into several large, spreading branches forming an irregular, rounded, or flat-topped crown. The leaves are alternate, compound, fifteen to thirty inches long, composed of eleven to seventeen leaflets borne in pairs on a stout, hairy stem. The leaflets are sharply pointed, lance-shaped, yellowish-green, rough above, and paler and hairy below. The fruit, ripe in October, is an oblong, rough, sharply ridged nut, with a sweet, oily kernel which is enclosed in a thick, sticky, hairy, greenish husk, turning brown at maturity.

Both the sap from the tree and the fruit were sought after by the Indians, from whom the early settlers learned to use them. In an old French recipe book, we found a method of pickling the butternut fruit when half grown.

If you can push a knitting needle through the pale green, fuzzy fruit, it is time to pickle them. The nuts, hanging in clusters, are harvested and placed in a solution of vinegar, sugar, and spices. It is claimed that the butternut goes rancid quickly but I remember, as a young boy, gathering the nuts in the fall and spreading them out on a large tarpaulin in the barn to dry. Then they were stored in fine, dry sand in barrels and used all winter long.

PICKLED GREEN BUTTERNUTS

2 pounds green butternuts	1 lemon, sliced
4 cups sugar	1 teaspoon whole cloves
3 cups vinegar	1 teaspoon allspice
1¹/₂ cups water	1 teaspoon ginger
	3 cinnamon sticks

Place the green butternuts in a kettle, pour boiling water over them, and allow to stand for 5 minutes. Remove the butternuts one by one, and, with a stiff brush, remove all the fuzz from the husks.

In a large stainless steel or enamel kettle, combine the water and sugar and bring to a boil to dissolve the sugar. Add vinegar, cloves, allspice, and ginger, tied together in a cheesecloth bag, and bring back to the boil.

Butternut

Lower the heat, add the lemon, and simmer for at least 10 minutes. Add the butternuts and simmer for an additional 10 minutes.

In the meantime, prepare several sterilized glass jars. Break the cinnamon sticks into inch-long pieces and place one in each jar. Remove the butternuts from the kettle with a slotted spoon and fill each jar to three-quarters full. Pour the cooking liquid over the butternuts so that they are covered. Seal with new rubber rings and screw down the lids while the juice is still hot. Let stand at room temperature; then store in a cool place.

CREAM BUTTERNUT FILLING FOR CAKES OR TARTS

2 cups maple syrup $^1/_2$ cup butternuts, chopped
2 tablespoons cream

Cook the maple syrup in the top of a double boiler until it almost threads. Stirring constantly, add cream and butternuts and bring to the boiling point. Beat vigorously until the mixture begins to thicken. If it is to be used for filling in tarts, allow to thicken considerably.

BUTTERNUT ROLLS

$^1/_2$ cup butternuts, chopped $^1/_3$ cup butter
1 tablespoon flour   2 tablespoons cream
$^1/_2$ cup sugar

In a 2-quart saucepan mix all the ingredients and simmer for 5 minutes. Butter a baking sheet carefully and dust with flour. Place spoonfuls of batter on the sheet, leaving plenty of space around each as they will spread considerably. Bake in 400°F oven until golden brown. Loosen from the sheet with a sharp knife and roll around a wooden spoon handle when lukewarm.

HICKORY *(Carya)*

The hickories are confined mostly to the hardwood forests of the eastern United States and Canada. We have twenty species of this stately tree in North America and five are found in Canada — Bitternut hickory *(Carya cordiformis)* with a thin-shelled, astringent nut; Shagbark hickory *(Carya ovata)* with a thin-shelled, sweet edible nut; Pignut hickory *(Carya glabra)* with a bitter, slightly flattened nut, less good for eating; Mockernut hickory *(Carya tomentosa)* with a sweet edible nut, somewhat resembling the Pignut and with which it is often confused.

The two edible hickory nuts are interchangeable in food preparation.

SHAGBARK HICKORY *(Carya ovata)*

The shagbark hickory, the largest of the species, reaches a height of sixty to eighty feet, with a diameter of up to two feet. When growing in dense stands the trunk is straight, topped by a small, flat crown. In the open the trunk is not as tall and divides into short, stout, spreading limbs. In Canada the Shagbark is found along the St. Lawrence Valley, from the Ottawa River to Lake Huron. In the United States it ranges from New England westward to Minnesota and southward to Florida and Texas. The leaves are alternate, compound, eight to fourteen inches long, composed of five leaflets borne in pairs on a strong, grooved, hairy stem.

The leaflets are widest at the middle, sharply pointed and toothed, dark yellowish-green above, paler and often hairy underneath. The fruit is a round, thin-shelled, sweet, edible, whitish nut. It is enclosed in a thick, dark, reddish-brown husk. It is ready for harvesting by the middle of October.

MOCKERNUT HICKORY *(Carya tomentosa)*

The Mockernut hickory tree is comparatively rare in Canada but is found from eastern Massachusetts to southern Ontario and Nebraska, south to Florida and Texas. It grows on a wide variety of soils, but thrives best on rich, well-drained slopes. The leaves are alternate and compound, eight to ten inches long, composed of seven to nine leaflets borne in pairs on a grooved, hairy stem. The leaflets are sharply pointed, dark shiny green above, paler and hairy below, and fragrant when crushed.

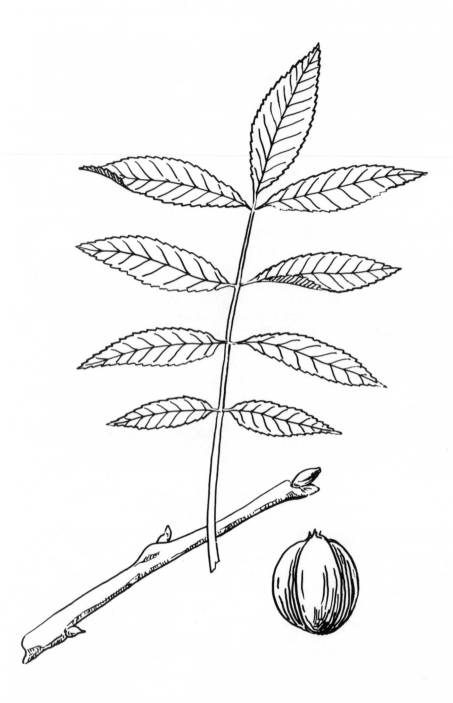

Hickory

The nut is large, but the shell is the thickest of all the hickories. It is so thick that, when opened, the small size of the kernel is disappointing. The name more than likely comes from the early New York Dutch word "moker noot" which means heavy hammer nut. The nuts from these two trees are, to my taste, the best for cooking purposes. Although all the hickory nuts are edible, some taste bitter and acid.

HICKORY NUT COOKIES

3¹/₂ cups flour
¹/₂ teaspoon salt
2 teaspoons baking powder
1 teaspoon baking soda
2 cups hickory nuts, finely
   chopped

2 eggs
1 cup sugar
1 cup shortening
¹/₄ cup whipping cream

In a large mixing bowl sift the flour, salt, baking powder, and soda together. In another bowl beat the eggs until bright yellow. Add the sugar, beat for another few minutes, and then stir in the chopped nuts.

Add the flour mixture to the eggs and knead lightly until the dough is flexible. Roll out on a floured board to about a quarter of an inch thickness. Cut with a cookie cutter and bake in a 400°F oven until golden brown.

HICKORY BONBONS

1 cup butter
1 cup fine sugar
1¹/₂ cups flour
¹/₄ cup cream

1 cup rolled oats
1 cup hickory nuts, chopped
¹/₄ teaspoon salt
1 teaspoon vanilla

In a large mixing bowl whip the butter until creamy. Add the sugar, flour, cream, vanilla, and the chopped hickory nuts. The dough will be stiff. Form into small balls, place on a greased cookie sheet, and bake in a 300°F oven for 20 minutes. Roll in powdered sugar while still warm.

TEATIME HICKORY TASSIES

1 3-ounce package cream
  cheese

1 cup flour
$^1/_2$ cup soft butter

Place the cream cheese and butter in a large mixing bowl and soften at room temperature. With a rotary beater blend the mixture well, adding the flour a little at a time. Chill slightly; form into 1-inch balls, and place in ungreased, small muffin cups, pressing the dough to the bottom and sides firmly. Set aside.

Filling

1 egg
$^3/_4$ cup brown sugar
1 tablespoon butter

$^1/_4$ teaspoon salt
1 cup hickory nuts, chopped

Beat together the egg, sugar, and butter until creamy and smooth. Distribute half the nuts in the pastry-lined muffin cups, add the egg mixture, and top with the remaining hickory nuts. Bake at 325°F for 30 minutes or until the filling is set. Cool and remove from the muffin cups.

BAKED HICKORY CUSTARD

3 eggs
$^1/_4$ cup sugar
$^1/_4$ teaspoon salt
$^1/_2$ teaspoon nutmeg

$^1/_4$ teaspoon vanilla
2 cups scalded milk
1 cup hickory nuts, chopped

Beat the eggs, sugar, salt, nutmeg, and vanilla for about 5 minutes; then slowly add the scalded milk a little at a time. When smooth and creamy, add the chopped hickory nuts. Pour into a baking dish, set in a pan of hot water in a 325°F oven for about 45 minutes. Serve with whipped cream.

BEECH *(Fagus grandifolia)*

The beech is medium to large in size, reaching a height of eighty feet and a diameter of four feet. The trunk is usually straight and erect when grown in a dense stand, and rises to a good height before branching into a broad shallow crown. If found on poor sites or in the open, it's a much less imposing tree — shorter and crooked, and breaking up into a dense, massive crown of wide-spreading branches just a couple of feet from the ground. The leaves alternate and are simple, elliptical in outline, sharply pointed, with coarse, sharp, inward-curving teeth two and a half to four inches long. They are dark blue-green above, paler below. The fruit, which ripens in late fall, is a three-cornered, pointed, shiny brown nut about three-quarters to one inch long, usually in pairs in a prickly brown husk, opening at maturity. This tree is found from Cape Breton Island to the north shore of Georgian Bay and south to Florida and Texas.

The young leaves of the beech can be eaten raw or used as a potherb in early spring. The inner bark, dried and pulverized, was used by the Indians as an emergency food. The nuts are small and it takes a lot of patience to collect them, but the effort is worth it.

BEECH NUT FILLING IN ANGEL PIE CRUST

4 egg whites	$^{1}/_{4}$ teaspoon salt
1$^{1}/_{4}$ cups sugar	1 teaspoon vinegar

Beat the egg whites until they form unwavering tops when the whisk is lifted from the bowl. Fold in the salt and vinegar alternately with the sugar. Place in a well-greased pie tin and bake for one hour at 275°F. Remove from the oven and cool at room temperature. Return to the oven to dry out.

Filling

4 egg yolks	$^{1}/_{2}$ pint whipping cream
$^{1}/_{3}$ cup sugar	1 tablespoon sugar
1$^{1}/_{2}$ cups beech nuts, chopped	

Thoroughly beat the egg yolks with the sugar, then add the beech nuts and half of the whipping cream. Place in a double boiler and cook for 7 to 8 minutes or until the mixture thickens. Remove from the heat and cool. Cover meringue with the filling. Whip the rest of the cream and add the tablespoon of sugar. Spread over the pie, sprinkle chopped beech nuts over the top, and refrigerate.

Beech

TOASTED SPICE AND BEECH NUT CAKE

3/4 cup shortening
2 cups brown sugar
2 eggs, separated
1 1/2 cups sour cream
1 teaspoon baking soda
1 teaspoon baking powder

1 teaspoon cinnamon
1/2 teaspoon ground cloves
1/2 teaspoon allspice
1/2 cup flour
1 cup beech nuts, chopped

In a mixing bowl cream the shortening and the sugar, then add the egg yolks and the vanilla. Sift the flour, soda, baking powder, cinnamon cloves, and allspice together and add to the egg mixture. Stir well and add the beech nuts, mixing until smooth. Pour into a well-greased cake pan.

MERINGUE TOPPING

Beat the egg whites until they stand stiffly when the beater is lifted from the bowl. Add a little sugar and continue beating until smooth. Spread the meringue over the top of the spice dough and bake in a 375°F oven for 45 minutes.

CINNAMON ROLLS WITH BEECH NUT FILLING

1/2 cup scalded milk
3 tablespoons shortening
3 tablespoons sugar
1 1/2 teaspoons salt
1/2 cup water
1 cake compressed yeast

1 egg
3 1/4 cups flour
1/4 cup sugar
3 teaspoons cinnamon
1/4 cup melted butter
1 1/2 cups beech nuts, chopped

In a large mixing bowl combine the scalded milk, shortening, sugar, and salt. Cool to lukewarm by adding the water. Then dissolve the yeast in the liquid and mix well. Beat in the egg, add the flour, and mix until well blended. Cover and stand for 20 minutes in a warm place. Preheat the oven to 375°F. On a well-floured board, roll out the dough to 18 × 12 inches. Spread with the melted butter, sugar, cinnamon, and the chopped beech nuts. Roll as for a jelly roll. Cut in one-inch slices and place in a well-greased pan 12 × 8 × 2 inches to rise in a warm place until double in size (about one hour). Bake the rolls for 25 minutes. Dust with confectioners' sugar and chopped beech nuts.

Chestnut

BEECH PUFFS

½ cup butter
2 tablespoons honey
1 teaspoon vanilla

1 cup beech nuts, chopped
1 cup flour
⅓ teaspoon salt

In a mixing bowl cream the butter and honey and add the vanilla and the nuts. Sift the flour and salt together and add to the egg mixture. Chill the dough for one hour. Form into balls the size of walnuts. Place on an ungreased cookie sheet and bake for 35 minutes at 325°F. Remove from the oven and immediately roll the puffs in confectioners' sugar.

CHESTNUT *(Castanea dentata)*

The chestnut, or sweet chestnut, was unfortunately attacked by a fungus disease introduced into North America from Asia about forty years ago. Many of the commercial stands have been destroyed, but you can still find a few old trees and numerous sprouts which spring up from the roots. A native of the East Coast, this large tree once grew from southern Ontario as far south as Georgia and Arkansas.

About ten species of chestnut are known — five native to North America but only one originating in Canada. The horse chestnut (*Aesculus hippocastanum*) on the other hand, is neither a true chestnut nor a native of this continent, although widely planted as an ornamental tree in our eastern towns and cities.

The leaves are alternate, simple, widest across the middle, coarse-toothed with sharp inward-curving teeth, six to nine inches long. They are dull yellow-green above and paler below. The fruit, mature in late fall, is a dark brown-shelled, sweet, edible nut about three-quarters of an inch long, borne singly or in clusters of two to five in a rounded prickly burr, opening with the first frost.

Why have we included the chestnut in this book when the tree is almost extinct? Maybe it is just nostalgia, or maybe hope that the tree will be reinstated on this continent so that our children will, at some future time, be able to enjoy roaming the wilds to collect this delicious nut.

WHITE OAK (*Quercus alba*)

The acorns from the stave oak or white oak were collected in great quantities by the North American Indians for winter use. This stately tree reaches a height of a hundred feet or more and can grow up to four feet in diameter. The white oak is probably the best known of all our oaks and it ranges from Maine, southern Ontario and Quebec, as far south as Florida and Texas.

The leaves grow alternate simple with five to nine deeply cut, rounded lobes four to nine inches long. They are smooth, bright green above and paler below. The fruit matures in late fall, with an edible sweet acorn half to one-inch long, enclosed for about a quarter of its length in a shallow cup of thickened knotty scales, slightly hairy on the inner surface.

I remember, as a young child, how in late fall we collected bushels of acorns for winter storage. The Indians usually ground the acorns until they formed a floury meal. The meal was placed in water to soak for a day or two in order to remove the tannin. The water was then drained off or evaporated away in the sun, and the remaining floury material was formed into cakes or loaves or mixed into other food.

I have found that if you roast the acorns before grinding, they have a sweeter taste. Also, if the ground meal is placed in water with a couple of pounds of birch ashes added, it will bleach the acorn meal and make it sweeter and whiter. Bread made from acorn meal is heavy and often has a bitter taste, but added to other flour it makes an excellent mixture.

OVERNIGHT ACORN MEAL BUNS

4 cups boiling water	1 cake compressed yeast
2 cups honey	¹/₄ cup lukewarm water
1 cup shortening	4 beaten eggs
1 tablespoon salt	2 cups acorn flour

Boil the water and honey for 5 minutes, remove from the heat, and add the shortening. Cool to lukewarm and add the salt and yeast that has been dissolved in the quarter cup of lukewarm water. Add the beaten eggs and then enough acorn flour to make a soft dough. The dough should be made early in the afternoon and left to rise until 5 or 6 p.m., when it should be kneaded down and left to rise until about 10 p.m. Form into buns, leaving space between the buns in the baking pans. Cover with a towel. Let stand in a warm place overnight and bake first thing in the morning in a 375°F oven.

White Oak

ACORN FLOUR BREAD

2 eggs
1 cup sour cream
1 cup honey

1 teaspoon baking soda
1½ cups acorn flour
1 cup walnuts, chopped

Preheat the oven to 325°F. In a mixing bowl beat the eggs and add the sour cream, mixing well. Melt the honey and add to the egg mixture. Sift the acorn meal and soda together and add a little at a time to the egg and honey mixture.

Grease a loaf pan and half fill the pan with the mixture. Place the loaf pan in the oven and bake for 1¼ hours, or until a tester inserted in the middle of the bread comes out dry. Remove from the oven and turn upside down on a wire rack. Allow to cool, with the loaf pan covering the bread.

WILD RICE AND ACORN FRITTERS

1 cup wild rice
2 cups cold water
1 cup acorn flour
1 teaspoon salt
1 teaspoon baking powder

2 eggs
¼ cup milk
2 cups vegetable oil for deep
  fat frying

Put the rice and water into a 2-quart saucepan. Bring to a boil over high heat, lower the temperature, and simmer for 10 minutes. Let the rice stand for at least one hour. Drain thoroughly and set the cooked rice aside. Sift the flour, salt, and baking powder together. In a large mixing bowl beat the eggs until pale yellow, add the milk, and beat well. Add the wild rice a little at a time, then combine this with the flour mixture and stir well.

Heat the vegetable oil in a deep, cast iron pan, hot enough that a piece of bread will brown in a minute. Drop the batter by tablespoonfuls into the hot fat and fry until golden brown, about 5 to 6 minutes, turning once. Drain on absorbent paper and serve hot with cranberry jelly.

DRY ACORN RUSKS FOR BUSH TRAVEL

2 cups sugar	$^1/_4$ teaspoon salt
1 cup butter	5 cups acorn flour
2 eggs	1 teaspoon almond extract
1 teaspoon baking soda	1 cup sour cream

In a large mixing bowl cream the sugar, the butter, and the beaten eggs. Add to the mixture the sour cream and the sifted acorn flour and soda. Finally, add the almond extract. Work the dough until it is light and pliable. Roll out in three 1$^1/_2$-inch-long rolls, place on a cookie sheet, and bake in a 375°F oven until light brown. Remove from the oven and cut the rolls into circles about three-quarters of an inch thick. Place the circles on a cookie sheet and set in the oven to dry at 250°F. The rusks are light in weight and easy to carry on a trip into the wilderness.

Edible Wild Fruits 3

JUNEBERRY *(Amelanchier canadensis)*

The Juneberry is shaped either as a bushy shrub of alder-like appearance which usually grows in clumps, or as small trees up to twenty-four feet tall. The leaves are elliptical or oblong, up to eight inches long and rounded at the base. The white flowers are arranged in racemes with longish five-petaled blossoms. The fruit is dark purple or black.

As with many other edible fruits, this plant is known by several names — Service Berry, Saskatoons, Shadbush, Indian Pear, or Sugar Pear. The Juneberry is found from Alaska to Newfoundland, California to the Gulf of Mexico, and Minnesota to Georgia. The fruit is a favorite food of bears, grouse, and pheasants. The pulp is sweet and surrounds ten large seeds. Don't remove the seeds when cooking as they soften and will give the fruit an almond-like taste.

The fruit was used extensively by the Indians and the early explorers who dried the berries by the bushel-load and saved them for winter food, used them in cakes or puddings, and in making pemmican.

PEMMICAN

1 pound dried moose, buffalo, or beef	1 pound beef fat or animal fat, rendered
1/2 pound dried Juneberries	

Hang the meat in strips, about 1-inch wide and 1-inch thick, on a rack to dry in the sun. Or, if you wish, cut the meat in strips and place overnight in the bake oven on low heat at about 125°F. Pound the meat to a pulp with a wooden mallet on a chopping block. In a large bowl place the pounded meat, the melted fat, and the berries. Stir well. Stuff into plastic casings or into a bag made out of cheesecloth. Hang in a cold place ready to take with you on wilderness trips or simply on your next camping trip. Pemmican makes one of the best concentrated outdoor foods you can take with you.

JUNEBERRY PIE

Pie Crust

$^1/_2$ cup boiling water	3 cups all-purpose flour
1 cup soft lard (not shortening)	$^1/_4$ teaspoon baking powder
1 teaspoon salt	

Pour the boiling water into a bowl and add the lard, which should be quite soft. Mix well, using a fork, until all the lard has melted and the mixture is like thick cream. If the lard is too hard to melt in the water, sit the bowl in hot water to soften it. Add the flour, salt, and baking powder. Mix well, using the fingers. Make a ball of the dough and place in the refrigerator overnight.

Remove from the refrigerator 2 hours before you want to use the dough. Roll out very thinly. This recipe will make one large 2-crust pie. Wrap what is left over in plastic wrap and freeze. It can be kept for months.

Filling

3 cups Juneberries	$^1/_2$ cup granulated sugar
2 tablespoons flour	1 tablespoon melted butter

Preheat the oven to 375°F. Pick over the berries, wash, and drain them. Place them in a 2-quart stainless steel saucepan and cover with water. Bring them to the boil, then lower the heat and simmer for 10 minutes. Drain and save the cooking liquid. Mix together the Juneberries, flour, sugar, and melted butter. Pour the mixture into a 9-inch pie plate lined with pastry. Cover with the pie crust, piercing the top with a fork to allow the steam to escape. Place in the oven for 25 minutes. Serve warm with whipped cream.

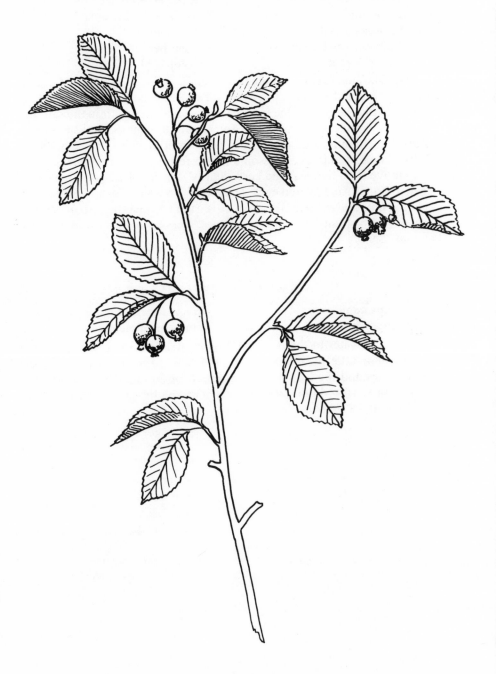

Juneberry

INDIAN JUNEBERRY PUDDING

2 cups dried Juneberries	$^1/_2$ teaspoon ginger
1 cup water	$^1/_2$ teaspoon cinnamon
$^1/_2$ teaspoon salt	$^1/_2$ cup honey
3 tablespoons butter	2 eggs beaten
$^1/_2$ cup corn meal	$^1/_2$ cup cold cream

Place the Juneberries in a small saucepan, pour the boiling water over the berries, and simmer for 5 minutes. Drain and save the cooking juices. Scald the milk in the top of a double boiler and stir in the salt, the butter, and the corn meal. Cook for about 20 minutes until thickened, stirring constantly. Add the berries, while continuing to stir the pudding. If it becomes too thick, add some of the reserved cooking juices.

Remove from the heat and cool slightly. Stir in the ginger, cinnamon, melted honey, and beaten eggs. Grease an 8 × 6-inch deep baking dish, add the mixture and pour the cream over the top. Set the dish in a pan of water and bake at 325°F for $1^1/_4$ hours. Serve with cold milk or table cream. Serves 4.

JUNEBERRY PRESERVES

2 cups water	6 cups Juneberries
4 cups sugar	3 tablespoons lemon juice

Bring the water to the boil in a 2-quart stainless steel saucepan, add the sugar a little at a time, lower the heat to simmer, and add the Juneberries and the lemon juice. Simmer for 20 minutes. Pack the hot berries in sterilized pint jars and seal. Process the jars in boiling water for 10 minutes. Makes 6 pint jars.

RED BEARBERRY *(Arctostaphylos Uva-Ursi)*

This evergreen shrub is found all over Canada, south to New Jersey, and along the entire length of the California coastline. The leaves are inversely egg-shaped and the base narrows to a short, downy stem. The upper surface of the leaf is shiny while the lower one is pale and dull. The flowers are white or pink and pitcher-shaped.

The fruit grows in short clusters and retains the cylix at the base of each fruit. Fruits are bright red and have a mealy taste. Their flavor becomes sour and acid, not unlike that of low bush cranberries, after the first frost, and it is then that the fruit is harvested.

SCANDINAVIAN STYLE BEARBERRIES

Gather enough berries to fill an empty wine or whiskey bottle. Add half a teaspoon of wine vinegar and fill the bottle with distilled water. Seal securely and place in a cool place, to be opened around Christmas.

Remove the berries from the bottle, drain thoroughly, and sprinkle with sugar when served.

BEARBERRY AND WILD APPLE BUTTER

1 pound dried wild apples, peeled and cored
2 quarts water
2 quarts bearberries
6 cups sugar
1 teaspoon cinnamon
$^1/_4$ teaspoon salt
juice of one lemon
$^1/_2$ teaspoon ground cloves

Soak the wild apples in 2 quarts of water overnight. Clean the bearberries and place in a pan with the apples and water. Bring to a boil, lower the heat, and simmer until the apples and berries are soft.

Put the pulp through a coarse sieve or food mill. Reheat and add the sugar, cinnamon, powdered cloves, and salt. Cook until clear. Remove from the heat and add the lemon juice. Spoon into sterilized jars and seal with wax or liquid paraffin.

BEARBERRY BANNOCK

3 cups all-purpose flour
2 teaspoons baking powder
$^1/_4$ teaspoon salt
3 tablespoons lard
2 cups cold water
2 cups bearberries

Using a large mixing bowl combine the flour, baking powder, and salt, first sifting the three ingredients together through a coarse sieve. Cut in

Red Bearberry

the lard and the cleaned bearberries, adding as much water as is necessary to make a soft dough. Knead lightly. Too much kneading makes the bannock hard. Flatten out the dough in a well-greased cast iron frying pan. Bake over an open fire or place in the oven for 30 to 35 minutes at 375°F until the top is golden brown. Break into pieces and spread bacon fat on top, instead of butter.

BEARBERRY TEA BISCUITS

2 cups flour	¹/₃ cup cold shortening
4 teaspoons baking powder	²/₃ cup milk
¹/₂ teaspoon salt	2 cups cleaned bearberries

Preheat the oven to 450°F. Sift the flour and baking powder together into a large mixing bowl. Cut in the shortening with two knives or a pastry blender, until reduced to peanut-sized pieces. Add the milk and the berries to the mixture; stir until both the dry ingredients and the berries stick together.

Turn out on to a floured board and knead the dough and crumbs together, flattening it out to a one-inch thickness. Cut with a cookie cutter and place on an ungreased cookie sheet. Bake the biscuits in the oven for 15 minutes.

OREGON GRAPE OR BARBERRY *(Berberis aquifolium)*

This bush grows from two to six feet tall. Because it plays host to the wheat rust disease, the Oregon grape is doomed in most states and provinces. However, the plant still survives along roadsides and on waste ground where it can find well-drained soil. In the spring and early summer the whole bush is one fragrant mass of yellow flowers. By summer, the oblong leaves, with their prominent veins on the underside, take on a glossy, rich green appearance.

The fruit is long and scarlet and grows in clusters. Watch out, when harvesting the fruit, for the long, sharp thorns at the base of the leaves. The Indians dried the fruit for winter use and made a delicious drink from the berries. The roots, too, were dug up, and used to dye Indian baskets and buckskins, and even the leaves were steeped as a remedy for rheumatic illness. Just like any grape harvest, the Oregon grape has good years and bad years. Today the fruits are collected mostly for jelly and jam. A year with the right combination of sunshine and rain is necessary. You simply extract the juice from the cooked berries with the help of a jelly bag or food mill. Then reduce the liquid until it runs from a spoon in the size of a silver dollar, or reads 220°F on a jelly thermometer. The Oregon grape is rich in pectin so there is no need to add commercial pectin. Pour into sterilized glass jars and cover with melted paraffin.

OREGON GRAPE AND APPLE JELLY

4 cups Oregon grapes	3 cups water
4 large wild apples	2 cups sugar

Pick over and wash the Oregon grapes. Quarter the wild apples, leaving the skins and cores and removing the stems and blossom rosettes.

Place the grapes, apples, and water in a 2-quart stainless steel saucepan and bring to a boil. Lower the heat and simmer until the fruit is soft and mushy. Transfer to a jelly bag, hang it up, and let it strain overnight. Measure the juice, add an equal amount of white granulated sugar, and bring to a boil. Lower the heat and simmer once again until the jelly thermometer reads 220°F. Pour into hot jelly glasses to three-quarters full and allow to cool. Cover with a thin layer of paraffin and store in a cool place.

Oregon Grape

OREGON GRAPE AND APPLE DRINK

4 cups Oregon grapes   **4 cups water**
4 large wild apples

Pick over the Oregon grapes. Quarter the wild apples, leaving the skins and the cores, but removing the stems and the blossom rosettes. Place the grapes and the apples, plus 4 cups of water, in a 2-quart pan and bring to a boil. Lower the heat and simmer until the grapes and the apples are soft. Transfer to a jelly bag and stand overnight. If you want a clear drink, don't squeeze the pulp. Bottle and store in a cool place. When used at a later date, just add water, sugar, and ice to taste.

OREGON GRAPE AND ROSE HIP JELLY

4 cups rose hips   **2 cups sugar**
2 cups water   **Oregon grape jelly**

Wash and clean the rose hips, removing stems and flower rosettes. Place the rose hips and 2 cups of water in a saucepan, and boil rapidly for 20 minutes, covered. Strain through a jelly bag overnight. Measure the juice and return it to the saucepan, adding the sugar, and boil for 5 minutes. Add an equal amount of Oregon grape jelly and simmer for another 5 minutes or until all the grape jelly is dissolved. Pour into sterilized jars. When cool, cover with paraffin and keep in a cold place.

BLACK CROWBERRY (*Empetrum nigrum*)

This bush is found in the arctic zones as well as in the mountains of New England and New York, north Michigan and Minnesota.

The stems are bushy-branched and reach a height of sixteen to twenty inches. The black crowberry is easily recognized by its leaves which are long and roll back until the edges meet. They are a lush dark green and crowded along the branches. The flowers are small, single, and purplish. The berry-like fruit is round, holds six to nine juicy seeds, has an acid taste, and is black or sometimes dark purple. Due to the large number of seeds, the fruit is seldom eaten raw but makes an excellent jelly or a refreshing drink. As the fruit itself is low in pectin, it's necessary to add extra pectin when making crowberry jelly.

CROWBERRY JELLY

2 cups crowberries
3 cups water
1 package powdered pectin

$^2/_3$ cup sugar for each cup of juice

Pick over the berries and place them in a 2-quart stainless steel saucepan. With the back of a wooden spoon crush the berries, then add the sugar and half the water. Let stand for at least an hour, stirring occasionally. Bring the berries to a boil and reduce to simmer for 30 minutes. Combine the pectin powder with the rest of the water and bring to a near boil, stirring constantly.

Add the pectin to the berry and sugar mixture and stir for 2 or 3 minutes. Pour into a jelly bag and allow to drain for a couple of hours, pressing slightly on the bag from time to time. Pour into sterilized jars, cover, and let sit overnight. Seal with paraffin and store in a cold place.

CROWBERRY MUFFINS

2 cups sifted flour
$3^1/_2$ teaspoons baking powder
$^1/_2$ teaspoon salt
3 tablespoons honey, melted

3 tablespoons shortening
1 egg, beaten
1 cup milk
2 cups crowberries

Sift the flour, baking powder, and salt into a large mixing bowl. Combine the beaten egg, melted shortening, honey, and milk, and pour over the flour mixture. Add the cleaned crowberries. Stir briefly until all the dry ingredients are moist. Fill the muffin tins three-quarters full and bake in a hot oven at 400°F for about 20 minutes. Serve hot with butter.

Black Crowberry

GRIDDLE CAKES WITH WHOLE CROWBERRIES

1¹/₂ cups sifted flour
3 tablespoons baking powder
2 tablespoons honey
¹/₂ teaspoon salt

1 egg, beaten
1¹/₂ cups milk
3 tablespoons melted fat
1 cup raw crowberries

Sift the flour, baking powder, and salt into a large bowl. Pour in the melted fat, honey, beaten egg, and milk. Stir in the cleaned crowberries, mixing just enough to wet all the dry ingredients. Heat a cast iron frying pan until a drop of water dances on it. Pour the batter by spoonfuls in small rounds on to the hot pan. Cook until air bubbles appear. Turn over only once. When the pancakes are golden brown, serve them with tart cranberry sauce.

CROWBERRY COOKIES

²/₃ cup shortening
¹/₂ cup melted honey
2 eggs
2 tablespoons milk

1 teaspoon baking powder
¹/₄ teaspoon soda
¹/₂ teaspoon salt
2 cups cleaned crowberries

In a large mixing bowl cream the shortening, then slowly add the melted honey and the egg. Beat with a wire whisk. Sift the flour, baking powder, and soda into the mixing bowl, adding the milk a little at a time. Fold in the cleaned crowberries. Let stand for 10 minutes.

Drop by spoonfuls on to a well-greased cookie sheet; bake at 350°F for about 20 minutes, or until the cookies are golden brown.

Salal

SALAL *(Gaultheria Shallon)*

Although this plant grows in abundance along North America's west coast, it is seldom found east of the Rocky Mountains. A cousin of the wintergreen, salal is an erect or partly prostrate wiry shrub, with dark, evergreen, leathery, ovate leaves. The flowers form in clusters and are whitish-pink, while the berries are black and hairy. It was the Indians who named this plant, which they found thickly carpeting forests, rocky cliffs, and ravines. The berries played an important role in the Indian diet. They were boiled down for syrup, or often dried and formed into cakes that were light-weight and easy to carry on hunting trips, as well as being extremely nourishing.

SALAL SYRUP

10 cups salal berries　　　　　**5 cups water**

Discard any berries that are bruised or discolored. Put them into a large stainless steel kettle and bring to the boil over high heat. Lower the heat and simmer for one hour. Empty the contents into a jelly bag and allow to stand overnight, squeezing the pulp from time to time if possible. Return the juice to the kettle and, over medium heat, boil down until the thickness of maple syrup. It tastes wonderful on pancakes.

CREAMY SALAL SYRUP PIE

8-inch baked pie shell	1 cup salal syrup
2 tablespoons butter	¹/₄ cup water
2 tablespoons all-purpose flour	¹/₂ cup beech nuts, chopped
2 egg yolks	

Melt the butter in a 2-quart saucepan; add the flour, stirring constantly. Beat the egg yolks with the syrup and the one-quarter cup of water, and add to the saucepan. Cook gently until thick and creamy, making sure that no scorching occurs, or, use a double boiler. Add the beech nuts and cool. Pour into an 8-inch pie shell. Serve topped with whipped cream.

SALAL DRIED CAKES

10 cups salal berries   **2 cups water**

Pick over the berries and discard the unripe ones. Place in a large stainless steel kettle and add the water. Bring to the boil, lower the heat, and simmer until almost all the water has gone. Remove from the heat and cool. Crush the berries with a wooden spoon. Transfer the pulp to a 2-inch deep baking dish and spread about half an inch thick over the bottom of the dish. Place in the bake oven at approximately 150°F overnight to remove all moisture from the fruit. In the morning, score into squares and leave in a warm place to harden. The cakes can be carried in your pocket to be chewed on during your wilderness trips or on a Sunday hike.

DRIED SALAL CAKES WITH CORNED BEEF

2 or 3 salal cakes   **1 tin corned beef, sliced**
¹/₂ cup water

In a large frying pan dissolve the dried cakes in the water. Add the contents of the corned beef tin, and heat thoroughly. Served with apple sauce or whole cranberries, it constitutes an easy meal on your camping trip or a time-saving lunch at home.

BOG CRANBERRY *(Vaccinium Vitis-idaea)*

This plant is known by such names as American cranberry, lingonberry, cow berry, low bush cranberry, and a score of others. The wild cranberry is considered one of the most important berries of the north, and its habitat ranges from Alaska to Newfoundland and as far south as Arkansas. Alas, many people find that it is disappointingly bitter and highly acid. Its smaller relative, the European cranberry, is a highly prized accompaniment to Scandinavian meat and pork dishes.

The bog cranberry's growth habit can vary but it is usually recognized as a low evergreen seldom more than ten inches tall, with leathery, glossy green leaves, and whitish-pink flowers. The berries are whitish-green before they ripen. They are perfectly edible, although they have a bitter, highly acid taste not unlike the musty flavor of the bogs where they grow! But cooked with sugar and spices, they are transformed into a different fruit.

At Christmas, in my home in Sweden, it was unthinkable not to serve a bowl of lingonberries sprinkled with sugar after the substantial Christmas evening meal.

BOG CRANBERRY JAM

2 pounds bog cranberries 2 cups water
6 cups sugar

Pick over the berries and discard any that are not ripe. Place the berries in a large kettle and add the sugar and water. Bring to a boil, lower the heat, and cook until the berries have split open, making sure that they do not stick to the bottom of the kettle. Cool and spoon into sterilized jars. Store in a cool place.

ROSE HIP AND BOG CRANBERRY JAM

1 pound ripe rose hips 6 cups sugar
1 pound bog cranberries 1/2 cup lemon juice

The best time to make this jam is after the first frost, making sure that the rose hips and the cranberries are ripe. Go over the berries, removing the remnants of the flowers from the rose hips. Crush them or push the

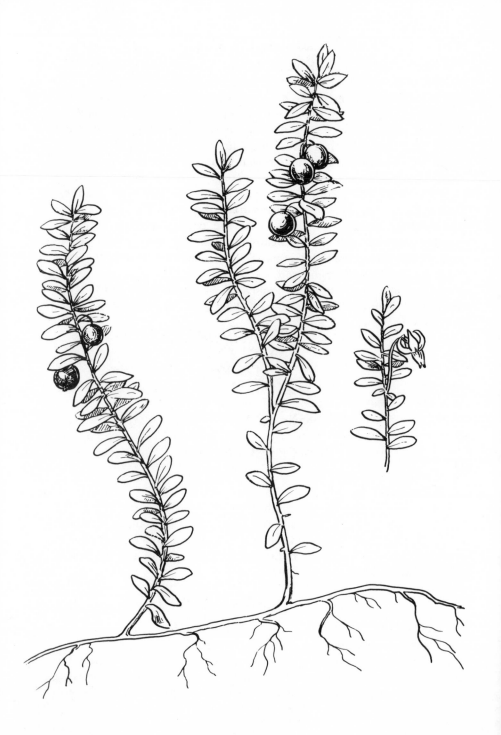

Bog Cranberry

berries through a coarse food grinder. Put the pulp in a large stainless steel kettle, add enough boiling water to cover the pulp, and cook for 20 minutes. Sieve the pulp to remove the skins and seeds. For every pound of pulp, add 6 cups of sugar.

Return the pulp and sugar to the kettle and bring back to the boil. Lower the heat, add the lemon juice, and cook for 15 minutes, constantly stirring to prevent the pulp from sticking to the pan. Turn off the heat and cool before storing in an earthenware crock or sealing in sterilized mason jars. Store in a cool place.

BOG CRANBERRY JUICE

3 pounds well-ripened bog cranberries	1 cup raisins
	3 cups sugar

Discard all the unripened berries. In a large mixing bowl stir berries and sugar together to make sure that all the berries are well coated. Fill empty liquor bottles half full of berries. Divide leftover sugar and juice between the bottles. Add 10 raisins to each bottle.

Fill them to the neck with water and tie a clean piece of cloth over each. Let the bottles stand in a sunny spot for about a month. When the month is up, shake all the berries and the juice out of the bottles into a sieve over a large mixing bowl. Press slightly on the berries to extract all the juice. After standing for 24 hours, siphon off the juice, being careful not to disturb the sediment in the bottom of the mixing bowl. Fill sterilized bottles and set aside until a hot summer day, when the juice diluted with water and poured over ice makes a slightly sour but refreshing drink.

BOG CRANBERRY AND RHUBARB CREAM

2 cups ripe bog cranberries	2 cups sugar
4 stalks rhubarb	3 tablespoons cornstarch
1 cup water	

Clean and peel rhubarb stalks and cut into one-inch pieces. Pick over the bog cranberries and discard any unripened fruit. In a 2-quart stainless steel saucepan, bring the water and sugar to the boil. Lower the heat and, when all the sugar is dissolved, add the berries and the rhubarb. Simmer until both berries and rhubarb are soft. Mix the cornstarch with a little water and add this to the berry mixture, stirring all the time. Simmer for 5 minutes, then pour into serving dishes and cool. Sprinkle with sugar and top with whipped cream.

WILD CURRANT *(Ribes triste)*

In 1930 botanists Britton and Coville recognized eighty-three different species of the *Ribes* family. The bush that we focus on here is the wild currant or swamp currant which can be found in the bogs and wet woods of Alaska, Newfoundland, Michigan, Wisconsin, and Minnesota. The leaves are similar to the familiar garden variety. They have three to five lobes, are smooth above and woolly white underneath. The flowers are greenish-purple, stand erect, and are borne on the old canes.

The smooth red berries, about a quarter-inch in diameter, are firm and sour. The Indians found endless ways in which to enjoy this valuable fruit and soon the early settlers, too, were discovering the currant's versatility for baking, drinks, and particularly for its mouth-watering jelly.

WILD CURRANT JAM

1 quart currants   **3 cups sugar**

Wash the currants and pick them free from the stems. Measure the fruit and sugar into a large preserving kettle and let stand overnight. In the morning, bring the currants to the boil over high heat, stirring constantly. Lower the heat and simmer. Test for setting as you would any jelly, by spooning a little on to a saucer and cooling on ice or in the refrigerator. If the jelly congeals when cold, it is ready to be poured into sterilized glass jars. Seal tightly, place the jars in the sun to cool, and store in a cold place.

WILD CURRANT JUICE

Wash the currants, leaving the stems on. Place in a large preserving kettle of stainless steel or enamel. Crush some of the fruit, adding just enough water to prevent the berries from sticking. Cover and heat slowly until the currants are soft and have lost all their juice.

Turn the purée into a jelly bag, or use a double thickness of cheesecloth, and drain overnight. Have several bottles sterilized and ready for use. Return the strained juice to the kettle. Bring to the boil, lower the heat, and simmer, skimming often. Add a little alcohol to each bottle, fill them, cork them, and boil them in a preserving kettle for 30 minutes. Cool on a rack away from drafts.

The juice can be used all year around for syrup or, mixed with water and sugar, it makes a beneficial drink.

Wild Currant

WILD CURRANT JELLY

1 quart wild currant juice   5 cups sugar

Put the currant juice in a 2-quart stainless steel or enamel saucepan. Add the sugar and boil, then lower the heat, and simmer for at least 30 minutes. Test for jelling by cooling a little of the juice on a saucer in the refrigerator. If it sets, pour into sterilized jelly glasses. If not, continue to simmer until the jelly will set firmly. Seal the jelly glasses with paraffin and store in a cool, dark place.

DRY SUGAR-COATED WILD CURRANTS

5 pounds wild currants   1 pound sugar

Pick over the currants, discarding any bruised berries. Place the berries in a large enameled preserving kettle and sprinkle the sugar over them. Simmer, skimming off the currants as they float to the top. Boil down the juicy syrup until it is quite thick and pour it over the reserved currants so that they are well coated. Dry them slowly in the sun or in a low oven. When completely dry, pack the berries in sterilized jars and tie a piece of waxed paper over the top.

When needed, cover with cold water and heat slowly to soften. The currants can then be used for pie fillings and for baking.

BLACKBERRY *(Rubus)*

A popular question on the nature trail is: How many different kinds of blackberries do we have? People are surprised that we can't give them a specific answer because even expert botanists have differing opinions as to how the raspberry and the blackberry families should be divided. One expert, for instance, identifies more than four hundred species. But, for all that, we *are* certain of one fact — they are all delightful eating. Let's make it easy by distinguishing between the erect, tall blackberries and the trailing blackberries or dewberries.

Rubus canadensis is the common northern dewberry found from the arctic to Virginia and Florida. A trailing vine, it grows in hedgerows, along roadsides, over stone walls, and sometimes even climbs trees. The leaves have three to seven oval leaflets which are sharply double-toothed.

The fruit is formed in small hemispherical clusters with large, juicy drupelets which, when fully ripe, are quite sweet and dark purple to black in color.

Rubus hispidus, the running swamp blackberry, forms a trailing or low arching cane, normally rooting at the tips. The leaflets, usually three in number, are obovate, broadest at the middle with a blunt tip, shiny, and stiff. The ripe fruit is nearly black. This plant grows vigorously throughout Nova Scotia, Quebec, down to North Carolina. When picking the berries watch out for small sharp thorns.

Rubus villosus is the common, tall bush blackberry, a variety identified by its stout canes, generously equipped with hooked prickles. The leaflets are three to five inches long, each having a distinct stem, the terminal one being the longest. The flowers look like clouds of white butterflies poised on hairy stems, followed by the fruit, dark purple to black, and grouped in long, loose clusters, with the lower berries ripening first. When ripe, the berries are very sweet. The common blackberry's terrain is similar to that of its cousin, *Rubus hispidus*.

Any one of these species of berries can be used for the following recipes. The amount of sugar may need to be adjusted, depending on the sweetness of the berry.

Blackberry

BLACKBERRY VINEGAR

This recipe may seem time-consuming but the first taste of this unusual drink on a hot summer day will repay your efforts.

6 quarts blackberries
1 quart wine vinegar

2 cups sugar to each
pint of juice

Soak 2 quarts of blackberries in 1 quart of vinegar overnight. Tie up in a jelly bag and extract all the juices. Pour this juice over 2 more quarts of blackberries and again allow to steep overnight. In the morning, strain through the jelly bag and pour this juice over the remaining 2 quarts of berries; repeat the process once more. Measure the final amount of juice into a large preserving kettle.

Add 2 cups of sugar to each 2¹/₂ cups of juice and boil for 20 minutes. Pour into sterilized bottles when cold.

Two tablespoons of syrup in a glass of water and ice make a refreshing drink. If you like it stronger, simply add more syrup.

BLACKBERRY CREAM

1 pound blackberries
1 cup sugar
2¹/₂ cups water

4 tablespoons cornflour
4 tablespoons water

Wash and clean the berries. In a 2-quart saucepan, bring the sugar and the 2¹/₂ cups of water to a boil, lower the heat and simmer for 5 minutes. Blend the cornflour with the 2 tablespoons of cold water and stir it into the berries. Simmer for another 5 minutes or until the juice thickens. Pour into 6 serving bowls and cool. Top with whipping cream.

BLACKBERRY JAM

8 cups ripe blackberries   **6 cups sugar**

Heat the berries in a large enamel preserving kettle, add the sugar, and bring to a boil. Simmer, stirring, until the mixture has a jelly-like consistency. Pour into sterilized jars and seal. If the blackberries have large seeds, squeeze part of the jam through a jelly bag. This jam makes a tasty filling for Swedish pancakes.

Swedish Pancakes

3 eggs   6 tablespoons margarine
2 cups milk $1/2$ teaspoon salt
1 cup flour

Beat together the eggs and half a cup of milk with a wire whisk for 3 to 4 minutes. Add the flour all at once and beat to a heavy, smooth consistency. Whisk in the remainder of the milk, the melted margarine, and the salt.

For the first pancake, lightly grease a large skillet and heat until it is very hot. Due to the amount of margarine in the batter, the skillet will need little or no additional oiling. Spoon 2 tablespoons of the batter into the middle of the pan. Quickly tilt the skillet back and forth to distribute the batter very thinly. Cook for only a minute or until the edges of the pancakes turn brown; turn, and cook the other side.

Keep the pancakes warm on a hot platter in a low oven. To serve, spread a spoonful of blackberry jam in the middle of the pancake. Roll up, sprinkle with sugar, and serve while hot.

OLD-STYLE BLACKBERRY WINE

4 quarts cleaned blackberries   2 pounds sugar
1 quart boiling water

Bruise the berries in a large preserving kettle. Add the water and allow to soak for 24 hours, stirring occasionally. Strain off the liquid, dissolve the sugar in the juice, then pour into a cask, and cork tightly. Let stand undisturbed for at least 3 months. Siphon off the wine into sterilized bottles and it will be just right for Christmas.

THIMBLEBERRIES or SALMON-BERRIES *(Rubus parviflorus)*

This thornless relative of the rose family grows six or more feet high in open woods and thickets from western Ontario to northern Minnesota and thrives from Alaska to California. The large, deeply cut leaves are much like maple leaves. White flowers bloom in terminal clusters.

The large red fruit, resembling a sewing thimble, is superb for jams and jellies, and memories of pies filled with thimbleberry jam or fruit linger persistently. The method for thimbleberry jam and jelly-making is the same as in the blackberry recipes.

THIMBLEBERRY PUDDING

1¹/₂ pounds fresh thimbleberries	2 tablespoons powdered arrowroot
2 tablespoons sugar	¹/₄ cup cold water
¹/₂ cup light table cream	slivered almonds

Remove any hulls from the fresh berries. Rinse them briefly in a sieve, drain, spread the fruit on paper towels, and pat dry. Cut the berries into quarters and blend in an electric blender at high speed for a minute or until they are puréed. Alternately, you can rub the fresh berries through a fine sieve set over a large mixing bowl.

Place the berry purée in a 1¹/₂-quart enamel or stainless steel saucepan and stir in the sugar. Bring to a boil over high heat, stirring constantly. Mix the 2 tablespoons of arrowroot and the cold water to a smooth paste, and stir into the pan. Without boiling, let the mixture come to a slow simmer and thicken.

Pour into individual serving bowls. Chill for at least 2 hours before serving. Sprinkle the top with a few slivers of almonds and top with cream. Serves 6.

PASTRY CONES FILLED WITH WHIPPED CREAM AND THIMBLEBERRIES

2 eggs	1 cup chilled heavy cream
¹/₃ cup superfine sugar	1 tablespoon sugar
4 tablespoons flour	1 teaspoon vanilla
2 tablespoons soft butter	1 cup thimbleberries

Preheat the oven to 400°F. In a large mixing bowl beat together the eggs and sugar until they are thoroughly combined. Now stir in

Thimbleberry

3 tablespoons of flour, a little at a time, and mix until smooth. Lightly grease a cookie sheet with 2 tablespoons of soft butter and dust with the remaining flour, tipping the sheet to coat it evenly. Turn the sheet over and tap lightly against the counter to knock off excess.

Place 2 tablespoons of the batter on the cookie sheet, and, with the back of a large wooden spoon, spread the batter out to form a thin circle about 5 inches in diameter. Set the cookie sheet in the middle of the oven and bake for 6 to 8 minutes, or until the circles are pale gold. Quickly lift the circles loose from the sheet with a metal spatula. Holding the circle gently in both hands, shape it into a cone, place the cone in a water glass for a couple of minutes, until it is cool, dry, and holds its shape. Keep cool until ready to use.

Just before you serve the cones, prepare the filling by whipping the chilled cream with a wire whisk or rotary beater until it begins to thicken. Add the sugar and vanilla and continue to beat until it is firm enough to hold its shape. Fold in the thimbleberries and spoon the cream and berry mixture into the cones. Perhaps the easiest way to serve the rather top-heavy cones is to place one cone in a small glass in the centre of a shallow bowl. Circle it with the rest of the cones, supported by the glass. Makes 16 cones.

THIMBLEBERRY SHORTCAKE

1 quart fresh thimbleberries	3 teaspoons baking powder
1 cup sugar	1 teaspoon salt
2 cups all-purpose flour	$^1/_3$ cup shortening
2 tablespoons sugar	1 cup milk

First, slightly crush the thimbleberries in a bowl, sprinkle with the cup of sugar, and set aside for at least one hour.

Preheat the oven to 450°F. Sift the flour, sugar, baking powder, and salt into a large mixing bowl, cut in the shortening with a pastry blender or use two knives. The mixture should be as fine as meal when you are finished. Stir in the milk. Place the dough in a greased layer-cake tin 8 inches in diameter and 2 inches high. Bake the cake for 20 minutes or until golden brown. Split the cake through the middle while hot, spread with margarine, and half of the thimbleberry mixture. Cover the top of the shortcake with the rest of the crushed berries and serve with cream while still warm.

Salmonberry

OLD-FASHIONED THIMBLEBERRY JELLY ROLL

1 cup thimbleberry jam

4 eggs

1 cup sugar

1 cup flour

1 teaspoon baking powder

Preheat oven to 400°F. Break the eggs into a mixing bowl. Sift in the sugar, flour, and baking powder. Mix well until smooth and creamy. Spread in a large, well-greased, shallow baking pan and bake for 15 minutes or until the cake is golden brown. Turn out on a flat surface, spread with butter and thimbleberry jam, and roll up while still warm.

Cloudberry

CLOUDBERRY *(Rubus chamaemorus)*

I can remember as a youth collecting these yellow fruits which grew in a swamp. The cloudberry, or baked-apple berry, as it is also known, is only four to ten inches tall, with leaves in pairs, simple, rounded, and slightly five-lobed. The white blossoms are carried on prickleless stems. The golden berries are small drupes borne on a flat receptacle. The cloudberry is found all over Nova Scotia, Labrador, and along the length of the New England coast. In the northern reaches of this continent it is a popular fruit for an unusual jam and as the basic component of a delicate liqueur with a rare flavor. As the berries squash easily, care has to be taken when picking them so they are not bruised.

CLOUDBERRY PRESERVES

4 cups cloudberries	4 cups sugar

Place the berries in a medium saucepan, squash lightly, add the sugar, and allow to stand overnight. In the morning, bring the fruit to a boil. Lower the heat and simmer for 15 minutes, stirring constantly to prevent burning. Remove from heat, and, with a slotted spoon, separate the berries from the juice. Set aside. Then boil down the sugar solution for another 15 minutes or until it starts to thicken. Put the berries back in the pan and, over high heat, bring to a boil. Simmer for a further 10 minutes, stirring all the time. Pour the preserves into sterilized jars and seal.

CLOUDBERRY LIQUEUR

4 cups cloudberries	1 cup water
5 cups sugar	12 ounces alcohol

Place the berries in a pot and squash thoroughly. Add 1 cup of sugar and let stand overnight. In a small saucepan melt the sugar in a cup of water, place over the heat, and boil. Cool when the sugar is dissolved. Place the berries and sugar in a jelly bag and drain, preferably overnight. Squeeze carefully in the morning to remove all juice. Pour equal amounts of the juice and sugar solution into a whiskey bottle and top it up with the alcohol. Shake well and let the liquor rest for a couple of weeks before using. Serve chilled in frosted glasses.

APPLE HALVES STUFFED WITH CLOUDBERRIES

1¹/₂ cups cloudberries   1 cup sugar
2 teaspoons sugar   1 quart cold water
²/₃ cup port wine   table cream
8 large apples

In an enamel or stainless steel saucepan, combine cloudberries, sugar, and port wine. Marinate the cloudberries for at least 12 hours. Pare the apples, cut in half, and scoop out the cores. In another saucepan put the apple halves, the cup of sugar, and the cold water. Bring to a boil, lower the heat, and simmer for 15 minutes. Remove the fruit with a slotted spoon and let drain. Place on a platter and fill the apple halves with the marinated cloudberries. Serve with a bowl of table cream.

CLOUDBERRY PUDDING

1 cup white sugar   1 cup cloudberries
1 cup sifted flour   2 cups boiling water
2 teaspoons baking powder   1 cup brown sugar
¹/₂ cup milk   2 tablespoons butter

Preheat oven to 400°F. Sift sugar, flour, and baking powder together, and place in an oven-proof dish. Add the milk and the cloudberries and stir until well mixed. Mix the butter and the brown sugar with the boiling water and pour over the pudding in the casserole. Bake for 25 minutes.

Edible Salads and Potherbs 4

ICELAND MOSS *(Cetraria islandica)*

In time of famine, this plant was often used by the Icelanders as a substitute for bread. Although its name would suggest otherwise, Iceland moss is a lichen but is often mistaken for moss because of its appearance. Its flat, erect, or leaf-like branches roll in at the edges forming a tubelike leaf, which is pale gray or brown in color, and when dried, becomes light gray.

Iceland moss normally grows above the tree-line in Alaska and northern Canada, but it can survive as far south as New Jersey and Pennsylvania. Lichens have often been credited with the difference between life and death by starvation for thousands of northern travellers and are a vital commercial commodity to the Icelandic economy.

Iceland moss has a marked rubbery texture during the summer but in the winter the combined forces of cold and wind dehydrate the plant and make it brittle. Soaking in water restores the lichen's more palatable texture and destroys its bitter, unpleasantly acid taste. A teaspoon of baking soda added to the water does wonders.

After soaking the moss, dry it and then crush and pound it to a powder. This powder can be used as substitute for flour when baking bread, or, when simmered with milk or water, will form a jelly-like gruel. Dehydrated in front of your fire, this gruel becomes firm and edible when cool. Often I have made a simple frying-pan bread by adding a couple of teaspoons of baking powder and half a teaspoon of salt to two cups of the powder, water to moisten, and cooked it in a greased frying pan.

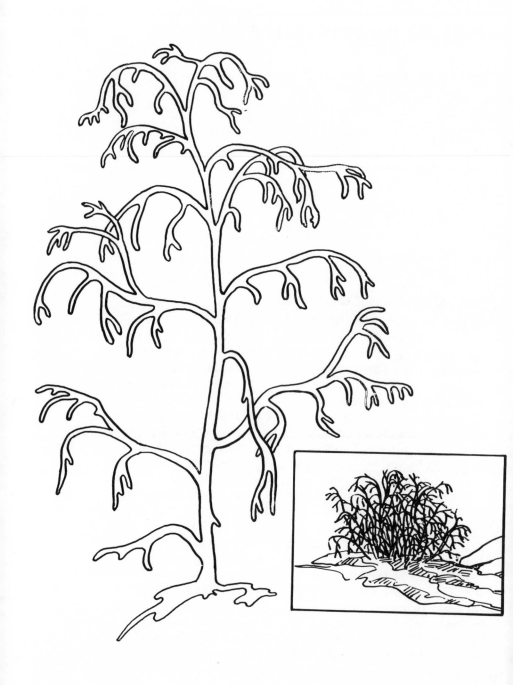

Iceland Moss

ICELAND MOSS PANCAKES

3 eggs
2 cups milk
1 cup Iceland moss flour

1 teaspoon baking powder
$^1/_2$ teaspoon salt
6 tablespoons margarine

Beat the eggs together with half a cup of milk, using a whisk. Add all the flour at once and beat until smooth. Add the remaining milk, melted margarine, baking powder, and salt. Because of the margarine in the batter, the skillet normally does not need greasing.

It's preferable to use a heavy cast iron skillet for cooking the pancakes. When the skillet is very hot, drop one tablespoon of the batter into the pan for each pancake. The edges will brown lightly after about a minute, so turn the pancakes over and cook for another 2 minutes. They should be served very hot, preferably direct from the pan to the plate.

DRY CRISP BREAD

4 cups Iceland moss flour
2 tablespoons shortening

1 teaspoon salt
1 cup warm water

Cut the shortening into the flour. Half way through, sprinkle the salt over the dough, and finish cutting in the fat until it is smooth and satiny.

Roll out on a floured board until very thin. Cut the dough into circular cakes with a hole in the middle. Heat a heavy cast iron frying pan on top of the stove. When the cakes are golden brown, dry them in the bake oven until crisp. Then thread the cakes on a cord in a dry, cold place until needed.

ICELAND MOSS MAYONNAISE

2 cups Iceland moss flour
2 teaspoons dry mustard
$1^1/_2$ teaspoons salt

2 teaspoons sugar
$^1/_4$ cup vinegar
$1^1/_2$ cups salad oil

In a large mixing bowl combine the flour, mustard, salt, and sugar until all the ingredients are thoroughly blended. Add a little vinegar and oil alternately, beating well after each addition, until the mixture is thick and smooth. Cover tightly in a glass jar and keep in the refrigerator for at least 2 days before using.

WHITE SAUCE WITH ICELAND MOSS FLOUR

1 cup milk
4 tablespoons Iceland moss flour

3 tablespoons margarine
$^1/_2$ teaspoon salt

In a double boiler melt the margarine, add the flour, and make a heavy roux. Add the milk a little at a time until the roux is smooth and creamy. Finally, add the salt and simmer for at least 20 minutes.

This white sauce has a better flavor than the traditional white sauce.

ROCK TRIPE *(Umbilicaria dillenii)*

Rock tripe is another lichen prevalent in the arctic regions but often extending as far south as North Carolina and Tennessee. Resembling a leathery, dark lettuce, the plant anchors itself to a rock, is about three inches in diameter, brownish-green above and brown or black below. It has a brittle texture in dry weather but is very flexible in the damp.

Rock tripe is certainly the best known in the far north of all the wild foods. The story goes that the explorer, Sir John Franklin, once escaped certain starvation by subsisting on this extraordinary plant. Perhaps he knew that the Indians often took advantage of its abundance when food was scarce. There are several species of rock tripe, and they have one thing in common — they are all edible. Although almost tasteless the rock tripe is very nourishing. As it adheres to rocky surfaces, it is naturally rather gritty so it must be washed several times before cooking.

Cut off the roots and simply prepare the rock tripe by roasting the leaves in a frying pan. Then simmer it in water for an hour or so. After it has been boiled, rock tripe tastes a little like tapioca with a slight tinge of licorice.

RABBIT HASH WITH ROCK TRIPE

3 cups large rock tripe
2 cups rabbit meat, finely chopped
1$^1/_2$ teaspoons salt

1 teaspoon pepper
2 tablespoons chives, finely chopped
$^1/_2$ cup rabbit broth

Wash the rock tripe leaves in several changes of water, making sure that all the sand and grit are removed. Roast in a large frying pan on the

Rock Tripe

top of the stove or in an open oven. When dry, crumble the leaves into small pieces. Grease a baking dish well and add the finely chopped rabbit meat, salt and pepper, the chives, and the rock tripe. Pour the rabbit broth over the ingredients and place in a 350°F oven for one hour, making sure that the dish does not dry out. If you wish, cover it for the first 40 minutes, then remove the cover and allow to brown.

JELLIED SQUIRREL IN ROCK TRIPE

2 cups rock tripe
1 cup water
2 cups rabbit broth
1 teaspoon salt
1 teaspoon vinegar

2 cups squirrel meat, finely
chopped
3 tablespoons fresh bulrush
shoots, finely chopped

Rinse the rock tripe leaves very thoroughly to remove all the sand and grit. With a sharp knife sever the root system. Place the rock tripe in a 2-quart stainless steel saucepan; add the water and the rabbit broth. Cover, and bring to the boil over high heat. Lower the heat and simmer for one hour. Remove the rock tripe, strain the stock through a sieve, and set aside. On a cutting board finely chop the rock tripe leaves and place them in a 3 or 4 cup well-greased loaf pan. Add the broth and the squirrel meat, sprinkle the vinegar over all, and stir well. Place the pan in a cool spot or in the refrigerator for one hour. Before serving, remove from the mold by setting it in hot water for a minute or so. Slice thinly and serve on Icelandic moss bread or brown toast.

FRESHWATER CLAM CHOWDER WITH ROCK TRIPE

2 cups fresh rock tripe
2 cups shelled freshwater
clams
1/4 cup salt pork, finely
chopped

1/2 cup wild onion, chopped
1 cup arrowhead tubers, diced
2 cups whole milk
1 teaspoon salt
1/4 teaspoon pepper

Wash the rock tripe at least twice, making sure that all grit and sand are removed. Cut off the root. Place the rock tripe in a 2-quart saucepan and cover with water. Boil, then lower the heat and simmer for one hour. Strain through a sieve, setting aside the fluid. Place the shelled clams in a 2-quart saucepan, cover with water, bring to the boil, and then reduce to a simmer for 30 minutes. Save the cooking liquid. Finely chop the rock tripe and the clams. Sauté the salt pork and the onions in a large frying pan for 15 minutes. Add the diced arrowhead tubers and simmer for 20 minutes, covered. In a 3-quart saucepan put the chopped rock tripe, clams, onions, pork, and arrowhead tubers. Pour into the saucepan 2 cups of the cooking fluid from the rock tripe and the clams, and simmer for 35 minutes. Add the milk and the spices and simmer gently for about 20 minutes. Serve hot with a dab of butter in each soup bowl.

JELLIED CARIBOU TONGUE IN ROCK TRIPE

3 cups rock tripe	1 teaspoon salt
1 medium caribou tongue	$^1/_2$ teaspoon pepper
2 wild onions	$^1/_4$ cup vinegar

Wash the rock tripe several times until the water runs clear. Remove the roots with a sharp knife. Cover the rock tripe with water in a 2-quart saucepan. Bring to a boil, lower the heat, and simmer for one hour. Place the caribou tongue in scalding water for 5 minutes, then remove the tough skin and all the base muscle tissue. Put it back into the water, add the onions, salt, and pepper, bring to a boil, and lower the heat. The tongue should be ready at the same time as the rock tripe.

Remove the rock tripe from the heat, strain through a sieve, and save the cooking fluid. Chop the tripe very finely. Remove the tongue, strain the cooking liquid, and set aside. In a 2-quart glass container, pour the two stocks over the finely chopped rock tripe and the tongue. Cool to room temperature; then place in the refrigerator for at least 3 hours or until jellied. Serve in thin slices on toast or on flatbread.

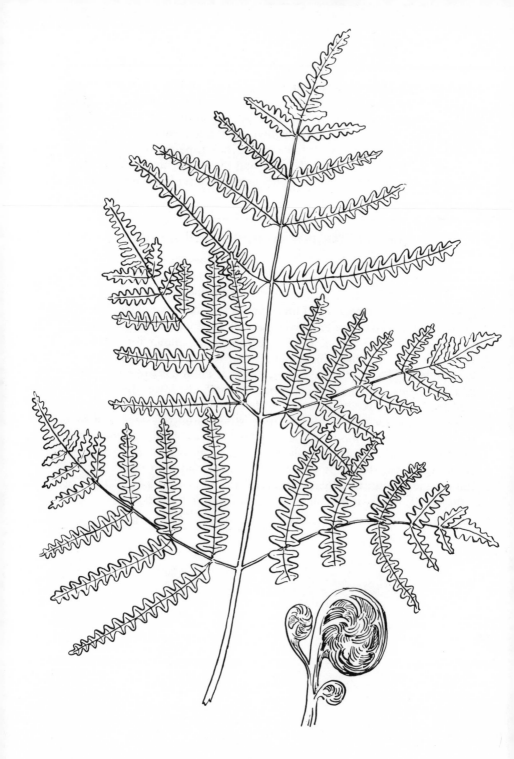

Bracken Fern

BRACKEN FERN *(Pteridium aquilinum)*

The bracken fern is the most widespread of all our ferns, covering almost all of the North American continent. You will find this fern in open spots in the woods, along roadsides, and in pastures. It can grow from eight inches to over five feet tall.

The stalk is stiff when mature and ranges in color from pale yellow to purplish-brown. The fronds are one to three feet wide, usually cut into three widely spread branches, each subdivided into leaflets. This plant is best gathered in the spring just as it is unfolding, and the tender stalks and fronds are used for potherbs or eaten, steamed, just as they are. The roots are highly prized by the Japanese for delicate soups. It is reported that in 1745, the Duke of Orleans, giving Louis XV a piece of bread made from ferns, said, "Sire, this is what your subjects live on." The North American Indians ate the fern as an emergency food, the tops raw or the roots made into a flour for bread.

CREAMED BRACKEN FRONDS

2 cups bracken fronds	$3/4$ cup heavy cream
4 tablespoons butter	$1/2$ teaspoon salt
3 tablespoons flour	$1/4$ teaspoon pepper

Place the curled fronds from the bracken fern in a 2-quart saucepan and add 2 cups of water. First bring to the boil and then simmer for 5 minutes. Allow to cool in the water. Strain the fronds through a sieve and save the cooking liquid.

In a 2-quart saucepan or double boiler, melt the butter and stir in the flour. Add three-quarters of a cup of the reserved fluid from the ferns, stirring until smooth and creamy. Cut the fronds in quarter-inch pieces, add to the saucepan, and simmer for 10 minutes. Stir in the heavy cream, salt, and pepper, and simmer until the bracken fronds are thoroughly heated. This dish goes particularly well with pork. Serves 4.

BUTTER-SOAKED BRACKEN FRONDS

3 cups small fresh bracken fronds	6 tablespoons butter
	salt and pepper

Wash and clean the fronds thoroughly. Pat dry with paper towels. Place a small bowl with serrated edges upside down on the bottom of a large saucepan. Add about one inch of water. Put a dinner plate on top of the bowl and place the fronds on top. Cover and boil for about 5 minutes. Melt the butter over high heat until it has a nutty aroma. Add the fronds to the butter, shaking the pan so that all the fronds are well coated. Serve.

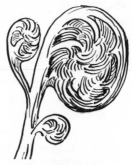

BRACKEN FERN ROLLS

2 cups bracken fronds	1 egg yolk
12 slices white bread	1 cup cream

Preheat the oven to 400°F. Wash and clean the bracken fronds and chop off the ends. Cut off all the bread crusts. Place the bread, one slice at a time, on a flat surface. Put 5 or 6 fronds on each slice and roll up tightly, securing with a toothpick. Whip the egg yolk and cream together until frothy. Spread the bread crumbs on a dinner plate. Dip the rolls in the egg and cream mixture, then roll them in the bread crumbs, and place them side by side in an oven-proof dish. Bake at 400°F for 15 minutes, the first 10 minutes covered with aluminum foil. When nicely browned, remove and serve hot. Serves 4.

BRACKEN FERN SOUP IN COLD BUTTERMILK

2 cups small bracken fronds	1 teaspoon lemon juice
3 egg yolks	1 quart buttermilk
$^{1}/_{4}$ cup sugar	

Wash and clean the bracken fronds; pat them dry with paper towels. Bring 3 cups of water to a boil over high heat and blanch the fronds for one minute. Remove, and, when cool, cut them into half-inch pieces. With a wire whisk beat the egg yolks in a large bowl. Gradually add the sugar, beating thoroughly. Add the lemon juice and the buttermilk, and continue to beat until smooth. Add the bracken fronds and stir so that the fronds are well mixed into the buttermilk. Serve in chilled bowls. A delicious spring and summer dish. Serves 4.

YELLOW OR CURLED DOCK *(Rumex crispus)*

The yellow dock, of which there are more than a dozen different varieties, is such a widespread weed that it is found in almost every open clearing, pasture, or cultivated field. This native of Asia and Europe was originally introduced to North America by the first immigrants, crossing the Atlantic in sacks of grain. It thrived on American soil and now spreads almost as far as the settlers themselves, from the arctic coast of Alaska to the southern United States.

The stout, smooth, dark green plant grows from one to three feet tall with all the leaves sprouting close to the base of the plant. The leaves are oblong, six inches to a foot long, and slightly heart-shaped. The edges of the leaves are wavy or curled and the leaves farther up the stem are similar in shape and appearance to the base leaves but much smaller. The plant bears greenish flowers arranged in whorls.

The dock provided a hearty green vegetable for the Indians. Some tribes of Eskimos and Indians utilized the abundant seeds to grind meal for bread-making.

The plant has certain distinctive qualities which make it an easy specimen to identify. Its taste is sour and bitter and the greens are often preferable mixed with other greens in a salad, and, because of their dominant flavor, require only a light touch with salad dressing. Salad leaves should be gathered early in the season when young and tender. I prefer them as a potherb, but, mixed with dandelion leaves and the tender tops of the black mustard, they make an excellent spring salad. In the autumn the numerous seeds can be ground into a flour for bread and cakes, with excellent results.

LAMB AND CURLED DOCK CASSEROLE

2 tablespoons margarine	1 cup curled dock roots
3 pounds breast of lamb, cut into 2-inch cubes	1 cup wild onion, sliced
	$2^1/_2$ cups beef stock
$^1/_4$ cup flour	1 teaspoon pepper
2 pounds fresh curled dock shoots	1 teaspoon salt

Preheat the oven to 350°F. Melt the margarine in a 12-inch heavy skillet until a light haze forms over it. Cook the cubed meat over medium heat, turning the pieces with a wooden spoon until they are evenly

Yellow Dock

browned. Transfer the meat to a mixing bowl. Sprinkle the browned cubes with flour and stir lightly with a wooden spoon until they are evenly coated and no trace of flour remains.

In a 5 to 6-quart covered casserole, arrange layers of the browned meat alternately with the washed and cleaned dock shoots. Sprinkle some of the finely chopped dock roots, wild onion, pepper, and salt over each layer. Repeat until all the ingredients are used, ending with a layer of dock leaves. De-glaze the skillet with the beef stock, scraping up all the bits and pieces stuck to it. Then pour the stock into the casserole. Cook for 1¼ hours or until the meat is tender. Remove the cover for the last 15 minutes. Serve with a dill sauce. Serves 4 to 6.

DEEP FRIED YELLOW DOCK BREAD

2 cups water	vegetable oil or bacon fat for
1 teaspoon salt	frying
2 cups curled dock seed flour	whole curled dock seeds

In a heavy 2 to 3-quart saucepan, bring the water and salt to a boil. Immediately remove the pan from the heat and pour in all the flour. Beat vigorously with a wooden spoon until the mixture forms a coarse paste that pulls away from the sides of the pan in a mass. Cool to room temperature.

Heat 2 inches of oil or bacon fat in a heavy skillet until very hot but not smoking. Using two spoons, form a small ball of dough. On a flat surface, press down in the middle of the dough with a spoon or cut a hole in the centre. Place the doughnuts in the fat, 2 or 3 at a time. Fry for 8 to 10 minutes on each side until they are a rich gold color. Drain on a double thickness of paper towels. Sprinkle the whole seeds on top of each one.

CURLED DOCK SOUP

2 pounds fresh curled dock	2 tablespoons flour
shoots	1 teaspoon salt
1 pound smoked beef	½ teaspoon pepper
3 tablespoons butter	2 quarts water

Wash the curled dock shoots thoroughly under cold running water to remove any sand. Shake the shoots vigorously, then chop coarsely.

Cut the smoked meat into about half-inch cubes. In a 3-quart saucepan bring the water to a boil, quickly immerse the shoots, and continue to boil for about 3 minutes. Reserve the shoots. Refill the saucepan with fresh water and bring to a boil, add the smoked meat, salt, and pepper; simmer for 30 minutes, covered. Strain through a sieve set over a large bowl. Reserve the stock.

Melt the butter, remove the pan from the heat, and stir in the flour. With a wire whisk, beat in the hot cooking liquid a little at a time. Return the pan to the fire and stir occasionally until it boils. Reduce the heat and stir in the curled dock greens and the smoked meat. Check for seasoning and simmer for about 5 minutes or until both greens and meat are heated through. Serve at once. Serves 4 to 6.

SPRING SALAD

2 cups tender yellow dock leaves	2 cups tender dandelion leaves
2 cups tender tops of black mustard leaves	2 cups watercress leaves
	$^1/_2$ cup salad oil
	1 tablespoon lemon juice

Wash and clean all the greens, making sure that the discolored leaves are removed. Tear by hand in about 1$^1/_2$-inch pieces into a large salad bowl.

In a small bowl beat the salad oil and the lemon juice with a fork or whisk until they are well blended. Gently toss the greens together, making sure that they are well coated. Pour the dressing over the greens and toss lightly. Stand in a cool place for 10 minutes or so and serve in chilled salad bowls.

WILD SPINACH OR LAMB'S-QUARTERS
(Chenopodium album)

This annual of the goosefoot family grows in gardens, roadsides, waste ground, dry woods, and barren land throughout the United States and Canada. The leaves are inflorescent, often red or reddish late in the fall. Stems are multi-branched and reach a height of three feet or more. The leaves are narrow, green or more or less white-mealy, broadly rhombic-ovate to lanceolate, and one-and-a-quarter to four inches long. The small, green flowers are arranged in spiked panicles and the seeds are black and shiny.

Many varieties of the goosefoot family are called wild spinach, mainly because the flavor is similar to cultivated spinach. Most of the twenty or more species native to North America are European or Eurasian strains and were imported by chance in pure seeds. A few were brought over by immigrants, cultivated in gardens, and eventually evolved into their present wild state.

The seed production is bountiful — as many as 75,000 seeds to a single plant. This, like the dock, is another seed widely used by Indian tribes in bread-baking.

PANCAKES WITH WILD SPINACH FILLING

Filling

4 tablespoons butter	1/2 teaspoon pepper
4 tablespoons flour	2 cups wild spinach,
2 1/2 cups milk	finely chopped
1 teaspoon salt	

In a medium-sized saucepan, melt the butter over moderate heat. Remove from the heat and stir in the flour. Pour in the milk a little at a time, whisking constantly. Season with salt and pepper, place over low heat, and cook until smooth and thick. Add the chopped wild spinach and simmer for a further 15 minutes. Cover and reduce to a very low heat, stirring occasionally.

Pancakes

3 eggs	6 tablespoons margarine
2 cups milk	1/2 teaspoon salt
1 cup flour	

Beat the eggs with half a cup of milk for 3 to 4 minutes with a wire whisk or rotary beater. Add all the flour and whip to a heavy, smooth consistency. Beat in the remaining milk, the melted margarine, and the salt. The batter should be very runny in order to have thin, light pancakes.

Wild Spinach

Place a crêpe pan over medium heat and grease once. The margarine in the batter will mean little or no additional greasing is needed. When the skillet is very hot, drop 2 tablespoons of batter in the middle. The pancakes should start to bubble almost immediately. After 1 or 2 minutes, when the edges start to brown, flip the pancakes over with a spatula and cook for about 2 more minutes. Keep the pancakes warm in the oven. When all the batter is used, quickly put about 2 tablespoons of the filling in the centre of each pancake and roll it up. Serve hot with a spoon of melted butter spread over each one.

SMOKED HADDOCK WITH WILD SPINACH

1 1/2 pounds smoked haddock	2 tablespoons flour
4 cups wild spinach	6 tablespoons heavy cream
4 tablespoons butter	1 hard-cooked egg

Wash and clean the wild spinach, making sure that all sand is removed. Chop very finely. In a medium saucepan cover the smoked haddock with water and bring to a boil. Reduce the heat to a simmer for 10 minutes. In the meantime, melt half of the butter in a heavy skillet and stir in the flour. Stirring all the time, gradually add the cream and the chopped wild spinach, and simmer for at least 15 minutes.

Drain the haddock and remove the skin and bones. Place the fish in the middle of a warmed serving dish, surrounded by the wild spinach. Melt the remainder of the butter and serve in a sauceboat with the chopped egg as garnish. Serves 4.

WILD SPINACH SOUP

4 cups beef stock	1 egg yolk
1 cup fresh wild spinach	1/2 heavy cream
3 tablespoons butter	salt and pepper

Wash the wild spinach thoroughly under running water. Melt the butter in a saucepan and add the shredded spinach. Simmer in the stock for 5 minutes, or until the spinach turns dark green. Reserve the beef stock. In a bowl, beat the egg yolk and cream, and add the spinach. Re-heat the stock in which the spinach was cooked, and, when hot, pour it into the bowl with the egg and cream, stirring constantly. Season to taste and serve at once. 4 servings.

WILD SPINACH CUSTARD RING

$4^{1}/_{2}$ cups fresh wild spinach 1 teaspoon salt
2 cups milk $^{1}/_{4}$ teaspoon pepper
$^{1}/_{2}$ cup cream $^{1}/_{4}$ teaspoon nutmeg
6 slices bacon 1 cup bread crumbs
3 eggs

Preheat the oven to 350°F. Wash the spinach carefully and then shred the leaves finely. Scald the milk, and, when cool, add the cream. Fry the bacon until crisp, drain on paper towels, and crumble it. In a large mixing bowl beat the eggs and cream until light and foamy. Add the salt, pepper, nutmeg, wild spinach, and crumbled bacon. Generously butter a 2-quart ring mold and shake the bread crumbs around in the mold so that they adhere to the sides. Add any left over to the spinach and egg mixture and pour this into the mold. Set it in a pan of hot water and bake in the oven for 40 minutes. Turn out on to a large dish and pour the same filling that was used in the pancakes into the centre of the mold, as a sauce. Serves 4.

POKEWEED *(Phytolacca americana)*

The pokeweed is a coarse, glabrous, perennial herb that grows along fences and hedgerows, and in damp woods. It can reach a height of four to eight feet. Leaves are oblong-lanceolate, branched, and from four to eight inches long. The flowers are greenish-white or suffused with pink. The berries are dark purple and about three-quarters of an inch in diameter. The root is poisonous and sometimes as large as a man's arm.

The plant can be found from the Maritime Provinces of Canada to Minnesota and south to Florida and Texas. Pokeweed is harvested when the first spring shoots appear, as later in the season the leaves become slightly poisonous.

To the Indians it was a familiar vegetable and medicine long before the advent of the white man. But it had other practical uses. The juice from the ink-berry, as it was called, made a perfectly good substitute for ink. It had other names too, such as pokeberry, poke, scoke, pigeonberry, and coakum. The early settlers could guarantee a supply of green salad shoots all winter long by digging up the roots of the pokeweed after the first heavy autumn frost, breaking them into six-inch pieces, and replanting the lengths of root in their root cellars.

Pick the shoots when they are not more than six to eight inches tall. The leaves make a good addition to a salad.

POKEWEED AND CHEESE SOUFFLÉ

1 pound fresh pokeweed stalks	³/₄ teaspoon salt
3 tablespoons butter	¹/₈ teaspoon pepper
3 tablespoons flour	¹/₈ teaspoon nutmeg
¹/₂ cup milk	2 eggs, separated
¹/₂ cup grated cheese	

Preheat the oven to 400°F. Peel the pokeweed stalks, wash them in cold water, put them in a pot, and add enough cold water to cover them. Simmer the stalks for about 15 minutes or until they are tender. Save half a cup of the pokeweed liquid. Arrange the cooked stalks in a 9-by-6-inch baking dish. In a saucepan melt the butter, add the flour, and then gradually whisk in the half cup of pokeweed liquid. Add the milk, cheese, and seasoning and cook, stirring constantly, until thickened and bubbly. Cool. Blend in the slightly beaten egg yolks, then fold in the stiffly beaten egg whites. Spread this evenly over the pokeweed stalks. Bake for 20 minutes until the top is delicately browned.

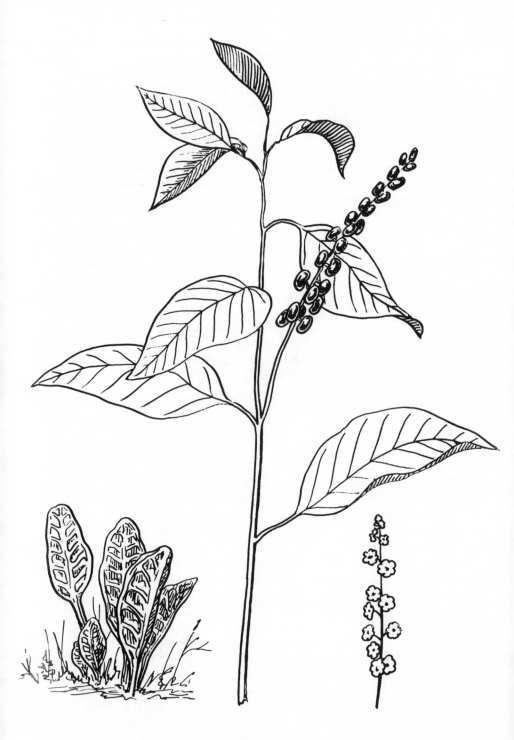

Pokeweed

FISH SOUP WITH POKEWEED

3 slices salt pork	2 cups hot milk
2 pounds fresh fish fillets	1 teaspoon salt
2 wild onions	$^1/_4$ teaspoon savory
2 cups pokeweed stalks	2 tablespoons butter
1$^1/_2$ cups hot water	$^1/_2$ cup pokeweed leaves

Place the pokeweed stalks in a saucepan, cover with water, and quickly bring to the boil. Reduce the heat and simmer for 15 minutes. Drain the stalks and save the water. Slice the pokeweed into 1-inch pieces. Place the pokeweed, sliced wild onions, and fish in alternate layers in a casserole. Add the hot water, cover, and simmer for at least 15 minutes or until the fish is flaky. Add the hot milk, salt, savory, butter, and pokeweed leaves without mixing. Cover the casserole and simmer for an additional 10 minutes. Serve piping hot. Enough for 4 generous helpings.

POKEWEED STALKS WITH HERB BUTTER

16 pokeweed stalks, about	1 tablespoon wild leek,
6 inches long	finely chopped
$^1/_2$ cup butter	1 tablespoon lemon juice
1 tablespoon parsley, chopped	salt and pepper

Wash and remove the skin and leaves from the pokeweed stalks. Tie the stalks together with string as you would asparagus, Cover the stalks with water in a pan; salt lightly, and simmer for 15 minutes until they are tender. Drain and set aside.

Melt the half cup of butter. To it add the parsley, wild leek, salt, pepper, and lemon juice. Pour into a small dish and cool to room temperature before placing in the refrigerator to harden. Just before serving, reheat the pokeweed stalks in a steamer. Arrange them on a serving platter and dot with the butter, cut into half-inch squares.

PICKLED POKEWEED STEMS

12 to 15 pokeweed stalks	2 cups vinegar
2 cups water	2 cups water
1 teaspoon salt	2 tablespoons sugar

Cut the pokeweed stalks into 6-inch lengths, remove the skin and leaves, and wash well. Put them in a saucepan with the water and salt and bring to a boil. Lower the heat and simmer for 15 minutes or until tender. Drain and place the stalks in a glass jar. In a stainless steel or enamel pan, bring the vinegar, water, and sugar to a boil, stirring until all the sugar has dissolved. Pour the liquid over the stalks, cool, seal, and refrigerate for at least 2 days.

Green Amaranth

GREEN AMARANTH *(Amaranthus retroflexus)*

This plant has many different names such as reed root, wild beet, and even sometimes pigweed, because it thrives in the fertile soil found around pig pens and livestock barns. It's possible that the amaranth originated in tropical America but today it is common all over the United States and Canada. The thick stem, usually without branches, can reach a height of six feet or more.

The leaves are long-petioled, ovate or rhombic-ovate, and up to four inches long. The flower stalks grow from the apex of the leaves and bear greenish flowers in long panicled spikes.

The shiny black seeds were ground into meal by the Indians and were a favorite ingredient in bread or porridge. The leaves, when picked young, have a mild flavor and are an excellent foil for stronger-tasting greens.

GREEN AMARANTH SEED HOT CAKES

2¹/₂ cups amaranth seed flour	1 egg
1¹/₂ teaspoons baking soda	2 cups soured milk
2 teaspoons salt	¹/₄ cup cream

Sift the amaranth flour, baking soda, and salt into a mixing bowl. Beat together the egg, the soured milk, and the cream; stir into the flour mixture, beating until smooth and well blended.

Place a heavy griddle over medium heat and put 2 tablespoons of the batter in the middle of the griddle, spreading the batter towards the edges. When bubbly, turn and cook on the other side. As they are cooked, place the cakes in a hot, covered dish until all batter is used up. When ready to eat, cut in half and serve with honey or melted butter.

GREEN AMARANTH CASSEROLE

6 slices bacon	6 cups green amaranth leaves
2 tablespoons honey	1 cup wild peas
1 teaspoon salt	¹/₂ cup sour cream
¹/₂ teaspoon pepper	

Preheat the oven to 325°F. In a large skillet, cook bacon until crisp. Drain, crumble, and set bacon and drippings aside. Wash and clean the green amaranth leaves, pat them dry, and shred. Stir the honey, salt, pepper, and the shredded leaves in the bacon drippings. Stir until they are well coated. Combine the amaranth mixture, wild peas, and bacon in an oiled casserole. Place the covered casserole in the oven and cook for 45 minutes until the peas are tender.

Spoon the sour cream over the top of the casserole, sprinkle with crushed green amaranth seeds, and serve. Serves 4.

HUNTER'S AMARANTH PANCAKE

10 slices fat salt pork
3 cups cold water
4 eggs
8 tablespoons green amaranth
   seeds, crushed

$^1/_2$ teaspoon salt
$^1/_4$ teaspoon pepper
2 cups milk

Place the salt pork in a large cast iron frying pan. Add the water and bring to a boil. Lower the heat and cook for 4 minutes. Drain. Cook the blanched salt pork slices over medium heat in the frying pan until well browned on both sides and all the fat is rendered. Don't remove any of the fat or pork.

Break the eggs into a large mixing bowl and add the crushed amaranth seeds. (To crush the seeds use an empty wine bottle. Spread the seeds thinly on a hard surface; roll the bottle back and forth until the seeds are crushed into a fine flour). Add the flour, salt, and pepper. Mix together until the batter is smooth. Add the milk and mix well.

Pour the batter over the salt pork and the fat in the frying pan. Cook for 15 minutes over medium heat, undisturbed. Lift the side of the pancake gently here and there, tilting the frying pan to redistribute the fat. Lower the heat, cover, and cook for at least 10 minutes. Turn out on a serving platter, bottom side up. Serve with whole cranberries.

MINER'S LETTUCE *(Montia perfoliata)*

Nature has countless wonderful ways of designing flowers and plants, but one of the most striking is miner's lettuce, whose unique feature is leaf formation.

This plant has several names; for example, Indian lettuce or Spanish lettuce. The Swedes call the plant winter purslane. Miner's lettuce is one of the most abundant spring plants down the west coast of Canada and the United States to Mexico, and as far east as North Dakota.

The stem springs from a bunch of basal leaves which vary greatly in size and shape from very narrow to kidney-shaped and even round. But their most startling feature is that half way up the stalk the single pair of leaves unite to form a disc or cup encircling the stem. At the top of the stem is a raceme of white or pinkish flowers. Generally, several stems rise from one cluster of basal leaves.

This plant was greatly sought after by the Indians and it was during the California gold rush that miners learned the Indian way to use this plant in combating scurvy — hence the name "miner's" lettuce.

The leaves are at their best early in spring when the fresh shoots are tender and succulent. As a salad green or potherb it is still delightful even after it has matured.

MINER'S LETTUCE SALAD

Dressing

1/3 cup salad oil	1/2 teaspoon salt
3 tablespoons white vinegar	2 tablespoons honey
1/4 teaspoon dry mustard	juice of half a lemon

Shake the oil, vinegar, lemon juice, mustard, salt, and honey in a bottle and leave for a couple of days in a cool place.

Wash and clean one pound of fresh stems and leaves of miner's lettuce. Pat dry with paper towels. Tear the lettuce in bite-sized pieces into a large salad bowl. Chill in the refrigerator for 30 minutes.

When ready to serve, shake the salad dressing well, sprinkle over the green lettuce, toss lightly, and serve at once.

Dressing

6 tablespoons vegetable oil	1/4 teaspoon pepper
2 tablespoons wine vinegar	1/8 teaspoon dry mustard
1/2 teaspoon salt	

Place oil, vinegar, salt, pepper, and mustard in a bottle; shake well and leave to stand until the salad is cool. Sprinkle over the salad and toss lightly.

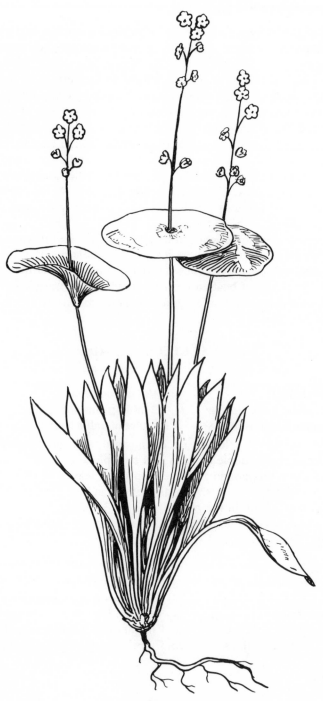

Miner's Lettuce

MINER'S LETTUCE AND RAW MUSHROOM SALAD

$^1/_2$ pound raw mushrooms   2 tablespoons chives
$^1/_2$ pound miner's lettuce

Wash and clean the mushrooms, and discard the stems. Slice the mushroom caps very thinly.

Wash and clean the miner's lettuce well; pat dry. Tear into bite-sized pieces using both leaves and stems. Chop the chives extra fine. In a salad bowl combine the mushrooms, lettuce, and chives, making sure that all the ingredients are well mixed. Chill in the refrigerator for 10 to 15 minutes while you make the dressing.

SWEET AND SOUR MINER'S LETTUCE

4 strips bacon, diced	2 tablespoons white vinegar
2 tablespoons butter	4 tablespoons honey
1 pound miner's lettuce	2 teaspoons caraway seeds
1 apple, diced	$^1/_2$ teaspoon salt
2 cups water	$^1/_4$ teaspoon pepper

In a 12-inch skillet fry the bacon until crisp. Sauté the finely shredded miner's lettuce in the bacon fat for about 5 minutes. Add the finely chopped apple, bacon, and water. Bring to a boil and simmer, covered, for about 20 minutes. Add the vinegar, honey, caraway seeds, salt, and pepper; cover again and simmer for another 10 minutes. Dot the butter over the dish and serve hot. Serves 4.

MINER'S LETTUCE AND MEAT CASSEROLE

$^1/_2$ pound bacon, finely cubed	2 tablespoons maple syrup
$^1/_2$ pound cooked beef, finely cubed	$^1/_2$ teaspoon salt
	4 tablespoons butter
$^1/_2$ pound miner's lettuce	grated cheese

Preheat the oven to 350°F. In a 12-inch heavy skillet fry the bacon lightly, then add the beef. Stir thoroughly. Wash and clean the miner's lettuce, pat dry, and shred coarsely. Place a layer of lettuce in the bottom of a 2-quart well-greased casserole. Put a layer of the mixed meat on top. Sprinkle salt and pepper on each layer. Continue with alternate layers of greens and meat, ending with a layer of miner's lettuce. Spread the maple syrup over all, dot with butter, and cover. Bake in the oven for about 20 minutes. Serve with grated cheese on top. Serves 4.

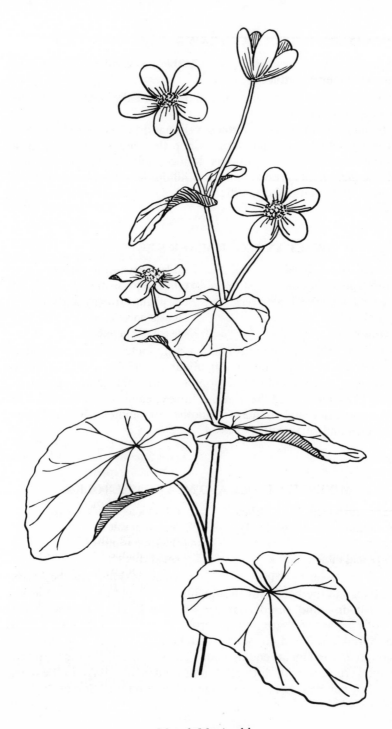

Marsh Marigold

MARSH MARIGOLD *(Caltha palustris)*

This plant is also known in many parts of the country as the cowslip because the size and form of the leaves seem to resemble the cow's calling card.

Found along stream banks or in marsh lands from Alaska to Newfoundland and right down to the tip of Florida, this is one of the early plants which so colorfully announces spring's arrival. The first settlers looked forward eagerly to its reappearance each year because it was one of the first fresh greens they tasted after the long winter.

The marsh marigold grows up to two feet tall and the shiny, heart-shaped leaves can be as much as ten inches wide. The bright golden blossoms, sometimes one and a half inches across, resemble a large buttercup. You will often read about this plant being poisonous. In a sense it is true. Remember, it must be cooked as a potherb, as only the cooking process definitely destroys the poison, helleborin. It is therefore essential that the leaves or stalks are never used raw in a green salad. However, don't let this fact deter you from enjoying the marsh marigold. But it is as well to remember that positive identification of all wild plants is an essential step if you intend them for the table.

MARSH MARIGOLD ROLLS

8 large marsh marigold leaves	1 teaspoon salt
2 pieces white bread, crusts	$^1/_2$ teaspoon pepper
removed	1 onion, finely chopped
1 egg	1 pound minced meat
1 cup milk	molasses

In a mixing bowl crumble the bread; add the egg and milk, leave to soak for a few minutes. Add the onion and the minced meat; work the mixture well with your hands or with a large wooden spoon.

Simmer the marigold leaves and water (to cover) for 5 minutes after they come to the boil. Drain, pat the leaves dry, and cool. Spread the leaves out on a board and spoon 2 tablespoons of the meat mixture on to each leaf, fold up, and secure with a toothpick.

Place the rolls side by side in a well-greased oven dish, sprinkle some molasses over them, and dot with butter. Bake in a 400°F oven, covered, for 45 minutes. From time to time baste the rolls with the cooking juices. Serves 4.

HOT MARSH MARIGOLD SALAD

10 large marsh marigold
  leaves
1 clove garlic, peeled and
  slivered
$^1/_3$ cup salad oil

$^1/_4$ cup red wine vinegar
$^1/_4$ teaspoon salt
$^1/_8$ teaspoon pepper
2 hard-cooked eggs, chopped
3 slices bacon, crisply fried

Place the marsh marigold leaves in a medium-sized saucepan and cover with water. Place over high heat, and, when boiling, lower the heat and simmer for 5 minutes. Spread the leaves on double paper towels to dry and cool to room temperature. When cool, shred the leaves into bite-sized pieces and refrigerate. Leave the garlic in the oil for about one hour, then remove it.

Just before serving, heat the oil, vinegar, salt, and pepper in a small stainless steel saucepan, stirring occasionally. Toss the hot dressing with the chilled marsh marigold leaves until they are well coated. Sprinkle the chopped eggs and the crumbled bacon over the salad and toss again lightly. Serves 4.

MEATBALLS IN MARSH MARIGOLD SOUP

Soup

8 cups shredded marigold
  leaves
2 pounds beef brisket
2 beef bones
2 wild leeks
2 quarts water

4 wild onions
$^1/_4$ teaspoon dill seeds
1 teaspoon dry mustard
2 tablespoons coarse salt
1 teaspoon pepper

Place the meat and the bones in a large soup kettle with enough cold water to cover. Add salt, and let stand unheated for an hour. Then cook over medium heat, first bringing slowly to a boil. Skim frequently with a large spoon. When the water is boiling rapidly, pour in a cup of cold water to slow it down; add the leeks, onions, dill seeds, and mustard. Cover and boil over medium heat for 2 to 3 hours.

While the soup stock is boiling, place a large saucepan on medium heat and add 2 quarts of water. Bring to a boil, add the finely shredded marsh marigold leaves, and cook rapidly for 10 minutes. Drain and set aside. Remove the soup kettle from the heat and strain the stock. Measure this liquid and add the same amount of water to the soup kettle, with the marsh marigold leaves. Bring to a boil over medium heat; lower the heat to simmer.

Meatballs

2 pounds ground meat	1 teaspoon salt
2 eggs	$^1/_2$ teaspoon pepper
1 cup milk	$^1/_2$ teaspoon anise seeds

In a large bowl combine the minced meat, eggs, milk, salt, pepper, and anise seeds. Mix thoroughly.

Form small meatballs, using all the mixture, and drop one by one in the soup. Bring the soup to a boil again for a few minutes, then lower the temperature and simmer for another 30 minutes. Serve very hot in large soup bowls. Serves 6.

SPICED MARSH MARIGOLD

1$^1/_2$ pounds marsh marigold	2 tablespoons honey
leaves	1 tablespoon vinegar
2 tart wild apples	$^1/_4$ teaspoon powdered cloves
1 small onion, finely chopped	$^1/_4$ teaspoon cinnamon
2 tablespoons butter	$^1/_2$ cup dry white wine
$^1/_2$ teaspoon salt	1 teaspoon parsley, chopped
$^1/_2$ teaspoon nutmeg	

Wash the marsh marigold leaves in cold water; pat dry. Slice the leaves finely; peel, core, and slice the wild apples. To a 2-quart stainless steel saucepan add the marsh marigold, apple, onion, butter, salt, pepper, and nutmeg. Cover with water, place over high heat, bring to a boil, lower the heat, and cover. Cook for 45 minutes.

Gently stir in the honey, vinegar, cloves, cinnamon, wine, and parsley. Cook for another 15 minutes, uncovered. This should be served as hot as possible. Good with any meat dish. Serves 4.

Horseradish

HORSERADISH *(Armoracia rusticana)*

Horseradish originated in Europe and Western Asia and became a legacy of the first immigrants to this continent who cultivated it around their homesteads. Since then the plant has gone wild all over North America. It prefers moist terrain and in places poses a problem as a weed. In some parts of the United States the plant is known as "sting nose" because of the nose-tingling, eye-watering effects of its white roots.

The straight-stemmed horseradish can reach three feet and sprouts from a thick root. The lower leaves are long-petioled and the blade is oblong, five to ten inches long and cordate at the base. The flowers, like most of the mustard family, are small and four-petaled, growing in loosely branched clusters. Now, of course, the horseradish mostly accompanies meat, but early in the spring the tender leaves are a very good addition to any green salad.

HORSERADISH BUTTER

1/2 pound butter	1/2 teaspoon salt
4 tablespoons horseradish, freshly grated	3 tablespoons white wine

Cream the butter with a wire whisk, or beat against the side of a bowl with a wooden spoon until it is light and fluffy. Beat the horseradish, salt, and wine into the creamed butter. Transfer to a serving dish and chill until you are ready to serve. Serve cold with fish. Makes 1 cup.

BRAISED CARIBOU FLANKS IN HORSERADISH SAUCE

1 1/2 pounds lean caribou flanks	2 leeks, sliced
5 tablespoons flour	1 1/2 cups beef broth
2 tablespoons salad oil	1/4 cup horseradish, grated
1 teaspoon salt	1/4 cup cold water
1/2 bay leaf	

Cut the meat into cubes and dust with 3 tablespoons of the flour. Heat the oil in a heavy skillet. Sauté the caribou cubes slowly in the heated oil until deep brown. Add the salt, bay leaf, leeks, and stir fry for about 5 minutes. Add the beef broth and horseradish. Cover and simmer in a tightly covered pan for 1 1/2 hours or until the meat is tender. Add to the stock the remaining 2 tablespoons of flour mixed smoothly with the 1/4 cup of cold water, stirring until thickened. Season with salt and pepper. Serves 4.

HORSERADISH CREAM SAUCE

¹/₂ cup sour cream   ¹/₈ teaspoon pepper
¹/₄ teaspoon salt   ¹/₄ cup horseradish, grated

Put the sour cream in a bowl, add the horseradish, salt, and pepper. Mix well and chill. Serve with fish or meat. Makes 1 cup.

FISH POACHED IN MILK WITH HORSERADISH SAUCE

1 pound fish fillets   ¹/₄ teaspoon pepper
¹/₂ teaspoon salt   2 tablespoons flour
1 cup skim milk   1 tablespoon white wine
2 tablespoons butter   3 tablespoons horseradish

Cut the fish fillets into serving-sized portions. Place them in a 2-quart saucepan and add the salt and milk. Simmer gently for 10 minutes, or until the fish flakes easily when tested with a fork. Carefully transfer the fish to a heated platter and keep warm.

In another saucepan make a roux with the melted butter and flour. Gradually add the milk that the fish was cooked in and stir until thickened. Add the wine and the horseradish, simmer for 15 minutes, then pour the sauce over the fish. Serve at once. Serves 4.

WINTER CRESS *(Barbarea verna) (Barbarea vulgaris)*

This is another plant of the mustard family that originated in Europe and was brought over by early immigrants as an impurity in seeds. It grows from Newfoundland to Florida, thriving in damp soil in fields, along roadsides, and on waste ground.

The glossy green leaves have four to eight pairs of lateral lobes. The plant blooms from late April to mid-June, with yellow flowers about half an inch in diameter, arranged in long racemes. The seed pods can be from one to three inches long, sharply four-angled on short stems.

Winter cress is often grown during the winter months. Back home in Sweden it was customary to pick the plant in the early part of December and my father would then protect the patch of cress with straw so that we could still harvest it, even after the snow had fallen.

Winter cress is often called scurvy grass, bitter cress, or Belle Island cress. Under whatever name, it is one of the best salad greens we have, if picked when the leaves are young and fresh. But many people prefer the mature cress when its bitter, peppery taste gives the salad more character. As a vegetable, it is delicious.

BAKED WINTER CRESS

8 cups winter cress	2 tablespoons flour
2 cups water	1 cup cream
1/4 teaspoon salt	1 egg yolk
4 tablespoons butter	1/2 cup bread crumbs

Wash and clean the winter cress, discarding all discolored leaves. Place in a saucepan, add the water. Bring to a boil, then simmer for 5 minutes. Drain the cress and reserve 1 cup of the cooking water.

Melt the butter in a skillet over high heat. Add the flour, some of the water from the winter cress, and stir until smooth and creamy. Add a little of the cream. Stir in the egg yolks and the rest of the cream. (You might need to thin the sauce with the remainder of the cress water.) Simmer for 15 minutes over low heat.

Butter a 2-quart oven dish. Lay some winter cress in the dish and add a little of the sauce; then another layer of greens and another layer of sauce. Continue this until all the ingredients are used. Finish with a layer of sauce. Cover with the bread crumbs. Place the dish under the broiler for 10 minutes. Serves 4.

SEAL CASSEROLE WITH WINTER CRESS

1 cup cooked seal meat, chopped fine	2 tablespoons butter
2 cups wild rice	3 cups winter cress, shredded
¼ cup wild leek, chopped	1 cup milk

Place the wild rice in a 2-quart saucepan, cover with water, and bring to a boil. Remove from the heat and allow to stand until cold. Drain and save the cooking fluid. In a bowl mix the seal meat and the drained rice. In a heavy skillet melt the butter, add the chopped leek. Cook for 5 minutes, then add the winter cress. Stir to coat the cress well with butter. Add the leek and cress mixture to the seal meat and rice, and put everything in a 2-quart casserole.

Dot with a tablespoon of butter and pour the wild rice water over the contents. Bake for 30 minutes at 375°F. Serve hot. Serves 6.

BAKED STUFFED RABBIT WITH WINTER CRESS

1 medium rabbit	3 tablespoons butter
2 large wild onions	1 teaspoon salt
4 strips bacon	½ teaspoon pepper
2 cups hot water	1 teaspoon dried savory
6 cups winter cress	½ cup leek, chopped

Skin and clean a well-hung rabbit. Wash thoroughly inside and out with warm salted water, making sure that all blood is removed.

Preheat the oven to 400°F. To make the stuffing, combine the finely chopped winter cress, 3 tablespoons of melted butter, salt, pepper, savory, and the chopped leek in a bowl. Mix well. Stuff the rabbit and sew it up.

Place the rabbit, breast down, on the rack of a roasting pan, with the legs folded under and secured with skewers. Arrange the quartered onions around it. Fasten the strips of bacon over the back of the rabbit, and secure with toothpicks. The bacon will prevent the meat from drying out while roasting. Put the rabbit in the preheated oven for about 15 minutes, then pour over the hot water, and lower the temperature to 325°F, continuing to cook until tender. Remove the bacon strips for the last 10 minutes to let the rabbit brown. Spoon the stuffing on to a serving dish as a bed for the rabbit. Serves 4.

Winter Cress

WINTER CRESS CUSTARD RING

4¹/₂ cups fresh winter cress	1 teaspoon salt
2 cups milk	¹/₄ teaspoon pepper
¹/₂ cup cream	¹/₄ teaspoon nutmeg
6 slices bacon	1 cup dry bread crumbs
3 eggs	

Preheat the oven to 350°F. Wash and clean the winter cress and shred finely. Scald the milk in the top of a double boiler; set aside to cool. Fry the bacon in a heavy skillet, drain on paper, then crumble it. In a mixing bowl beat the eggs until light and foamy. Add the cream, salt, and pepper. Gradually add the winter cress, crumbled bacon, bacon fat, and bread crumbs. Generously butter a 2-quart ring mold and pour in the mixture. Place the mold in a pan of water and bake for 45 minutes. Unmold the ring on a large platter and fill the centre with creamed winter cress.

SAXIFRAGE *(Saxifraga micranthidifolia)*

This perennial plant clings, with the help of a strong root, to wet cliffs and along mountain streams from east Pennsylvania, south to Georgia and Tennessee. The flowering stems grow from ten to twenty inches tall and are branched above the middle. The basal leaves are oblong, three to eight times as long as they are wide, and usually about four to eight inches long. The flowers are white with a yellow spot near the base.

This plant was much sought after by the early Pennsylvania Dutch as a salad plant. Traditionally, rural people have often called the plant Deer Tongue and it is sometimes confused with its cousin, the Indian rhubarb *(Saxifraga peltata)*, which usually grows farther west in the rocky mountain streams of northern California.

The leaves are deliciously tender from early May to the middle of June. As the season progresses they become bitter.

PENNSYLVANIA DUTCH SAXIFRAGE

6 cups tender saxifrage leaves　　　**1 tablespoon honey**
8 slices smoked bacon or ham

Wash and clean the saxifrage leaves thoroughly; shred into bite-sized pieces. Fry the bacon or ham in a heavy skillet until crisp. Drain on paper towels. Add the honey to the drippings in the skillet and stir until dissolved. Add the shredded leaves and gently turn the leaves, coating them with the honey mixture. Crumble the bacon into the skillet. Serve on buttered toast.

SWEET AND SOUR SAXIFRAGE

4 cups saxifrage leaves　　　　**4 tablespoons honey**
1/2 cup boiling water　　　　　**4 tablespoons cider vinegar**
1 teaspoon salt　　　　　　　　**3 whole cloves**
2 tart wild apples　　　　　　　**2 tablespoons butter**

Wash and clean the leaves thoroughly, then shred finely. Put them into a heavy skillet with the boiling water and salt, and cover. First bring to a boil, then simmer for about 5 minutes. Peel, core, and slice the apples. Add the honey, vinegar, cloves, and butter to the skillet, cover, and simmer for 3 to 4 minutes. Put the drained greens and apples back in the pan, and stir carefully until well mixed with the juice. Serve hot. Serves 4.

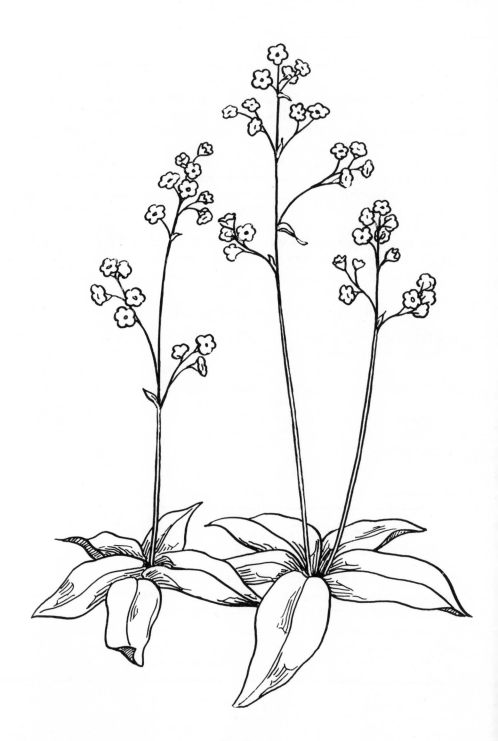

Saxifrage

CREAMED SAXIFRAGE

1 pound tender saxifrage leaves	¹/₄ teaspoon pepper
2 tablespoons butter	¹/₄ teaspoon nutmeg
2 tablespoons flour	¹/₂ cup white table wine
¹/₂ teaspoon salt	1 hard-cooked egg, chopped

Wash the saxifrage leaves, put them in a 2-quart saucepan, add half a cup of water, and boil for 2 minutes. Drain them, saving the water. Melt the butter in the saucepan, add the flour, making a heavy roux. Slowly add the cooking water, salt, pepper, nutmeg, and wine. Simmer. Finely chop the cooked saxifrage greens and stir gently into the saucepan. Simmer for 3 to 4 minutes until they are hot. Serve in a warmed bowl with the chopped egg sprinkled on top. For 4 people.

SAXIFRAGE SPRING SALAD

5 cups tender saxifrage leaves	2 tablespoons wild onion
2 tablespoons chives	

Dressing

1 cup mayonnaise	¹/₄ cup Danish blue cheese
2 tablespoons lemon juice	

Mash the blue cheese with the lemon juice and add a spoonful of mayonnaise. Mix until smooth and creamy. Add the rest of the mayonnaise. Place in the refrigerator to chill.

Finely shred the greens into a salad bowl, mix in the finely chopped onion and the chives, and chill in the refrigerator. Just before serving, toss lightly with 4 tablespoons of the dressing. Enough for 4 servings.

Prickly Lettuce

PRICKLY LETTUCE (*Lactuca scariola*)

The prickly lettuce is found in fields and waste places. It is originally a European plant but is now a familiar weed throughout the United States and Canada.

It is easily recognized by a row of yellowish spines along the midribs on the lower surface of the leaves, edged with fine, prickly teeth. The flowers are yellow, often drying blue, and are usually widely spread on a branching head. The plant is biennial and was once commonly substituted for lettuce. As a matter of fact, botanists today theorize that the lettuce we now cultivate evolved from this plant. The plant is dubbed the compass weed in some parts of the country because the sharply-toothed and tipped edges of the leaves twist towards the sun.

The leaves should be picked in early spring for a salad but can be gathered all summer long for use in cooked dishes. The sharp spines soften quickly when dipped in boiling water. I have found that this seems to seal in the freshness of the leaves and helps them to keep their color.

HICKORY SMOKED PRICKLY LETTUCE

4 tablespoons butter
4 cups prickly lettuce leaves
1 teaspoon hickory salt
$^1/_4$ teaspoon pepper
3 tablespoons whipping cream

Wash and clean the prickly lettuce leaves. Shred finely. Boil 3 cups of water over high heat. Add the prickly lettuce leaves and blanch for one minute; remove and drain. Melt the butter in a large skillet, and when the butter has a nutty aroma, lower the heat and add hickory salt and pepper. Then add whipping cream a little at a time, stirring constantly. When well mixed, add the prickly lettuce leaves, cover, and cook for 5 minutes over low heat. Stir to make sure that all leaves are coated with the mixture. Serves 4.

PRICKLY LETTUCE SPRING SALAD

5 cups shredded prickly lettuce leaves
2 cups maple sap

Wash and clean the leaves and shred into large pieces. Boil the 2 cups of sap over high heat in a large saucepan. Place the leaves in a sieve and immerse in the maple sap for one minute. Remove and drain. Cool to room temperature, then chill.

Dressing
1¹/₄ cup mayonnaise   ¹/₂ teaspoon salt
4 tablespoons maple syrup   ¹/₄ teaspoon pepper

Beat the ingredients with a wire whisk until smooth and creamy. Chill in the refrigerator. When ready to serve, toss gently with 3 or 4 tablespoons of dressing, making sure that the leaves are evenly coated.

FRESH PRICKLY LETTUCE OMELET

4 large eggs   ¹/₄ teaspoon pepper
4 tablespoons water   1 tablespoon butter
¹/₂ teaspoon salt

Blend eggs briskly with a fork; stir in water, salt, and pepper. Melt the butter in an omelet pan on medium heat, making sure that the butter coats the bottom and sides of the pan. After the butter has stopped foaming, pour in the egg mixture immediately. Stir briskly with a fork, letting the uncooked liquid flow to the bottom. Draw the setting outer edges toward the centre of the pan and run the fork around the edges. Slide the omelet on to a heated plate.

Filling
3 cups fresh prickly lettuce   4 tablespoons butter

Wash and clean the prickly lettuce leaves. Bring 3 cups of water to a boil in a medium saucepan. Cook the leaves for one minute, drain, and dry with paper towels. Melt the butter. Place the prickly lettuce leaves in the centre of the omelet, pour the melted butter over, and serve at once. Serves 4.

LATE SUMMER PRICKLY LETTUCE LEAVES AND HAM CASSEROLE

6 cups prickly lettuce leaves   3 tablespoons butter
1¹/₂ cups milk   3 tablespoons flour
¹/₂ cup cream   2 cups diced smoked ham
2 teaspoons prepared mustard   ¹/₂ cup grated cheese
¹/₂ teaspoon salt

Preheat the oven to 375°F. Wash and clean the prickly lettuce leaves, place in a bowl, and pour boiling water over the leaves. Allow to stand for 5 minutes, then drain thoroughly and shred. In a small saucepan heat the milk, cream, mustard, and salt, then stir in the combined butter and flour. Whisk the mixture until smooth and creamy. Fold in the smoked ham and the lettuce leaves. Spread the mixture in a greased 8-inch baking dish and sprinkle with cheese. Bake for about 20 minutes and serve straight from the oven.

SOLOMON'S SEAL *(Polygonatum pubescens)*

This relative of the lily family grows ten to twelve inches tall with slender, erect stems. The leaves are offset and elliptical to broadly oval with very prominent veins. Yellowish-green flowers grow in pairs on graceful stalks, bursting out from under the leaves. The plant is usually found in damp woods and thickets, from Nova Scotia to Ontario, as far south as Georgia, and west from Minnesota to Kentucky and Indiana.

The roots formed a starchy vegetable in the Indian diet. They were also boiled down to make a gruel, the water evaporated, and the residue used as a heavy flour in cakes and bread.

The early leaves, boiled and served like asparagus, are an excellent vegetable, but later in summer they become bitter and woody. I have found the leaves to be most palatable in casseroles or mixed with other greens in a spring soup.

SOLOMON'S SEAL CASSEROLE

4 cups solomon's seal leaves, shredded	1 cup hot milk
	1/2 cup mayonnaise
2 tablespoons soft butter	1/2 cup buttered bread crumbs
2 tablespoons flour	1/2 cup grated sharp cheese
1/4 teaspoon salt	

Preheat the oven to 400°F. Gently simmer the solomon's seal leaves in salted water for at least 15 minutes. Drain and pat dry with a paper towel. Spread the leaves evenly in an 8-by-8-inch baking dish. In a small saucepan cream the butter and flour, add the salt, and cook over low heat until thick. Stirring all the time, add the hot milk little by little. Remove from the heat and blend in the mayonnaise. Pour the sauce over the solomon's seal leaves and top with bread crumbs and cheese. Heat in the oven for 15 minutes, then broil until topping is lightly browned. Serves 4.

SOLOMON'S SEAL BREAD ROLLS

4 cups whole solomon's seal leaves	8 slices white bread
	2 tablespoons butter
1/2 teaspoon salt	1/4 cup grated cheese

In a saucepan cover the solomon's seal leaves with salted water. Simmer for 10 minutes. Remove the bread crusts and butter each slice.

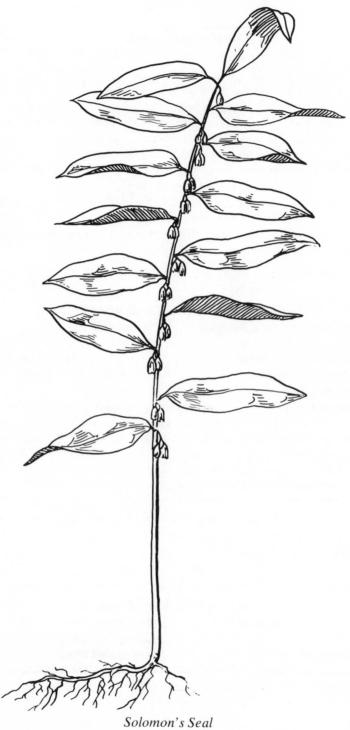

Solomon's Seal

Drain the greens thoroughly and cool to room temperature. Divide the leaves evenly, spread over the bread slices, and sprinkle with cheese. Roll the slices, jelly-roll style, and secure with toothpicks. Place the rolls side by side in a baking dish and toast under the broiler until light brown. Serve with the white sauce. Serves 4.

SOLOMON'S SEAL LEAVES IN BUTTERY SAUCE

4 cups fresh solomon's seal
leaves
1 teaspoon salt

4 tablespoons butter
1 teaspoon horseradish
$^{1}/_{2}$ cup sour cream

Wash and clean the greens, removing all the small stalks. Place half the leaves in a 2-quart saucepan over heat, and sprinkle with half the salt. Add the rest of the leaves and salt.

Pour on 1 cup of boiling water and cook for 20 minutes, covered. In a small pot melt the butter, and add the horseradish and the sour cream bit by bit. Drain the leaves, add them to the butter mixture, cover, and simmer for 5 minutes. Stir to make sure that all the leaves have been coated with the butter mixture. Serves 4.

HONEY-COVERED SOLOMON'S SEAL LEAVES

3 slices side bacon, diced
2 tablespoons prepared
horseradish
2 tablespoons honey

2 tablespoons lemon juice
4 cups solomon's seal leaves
$^{1}/_{2}$ teaspoon salt

Wash and clean the leaves, shred in small pieces, and set aside to drain. Place the leaves in a 2-quart stainless steel saucepan, add water to cover, and salt. Place over high heat and bring to a boil, lower the heat, and simmer for 15 minutes.

Sauté the bacon until golden brown and crisp. Turn the heat to low and add the horseradish, honey, and lemon juice, stirring well to mix all the ingredients; add the shredded leaves. Cover and heat thoroughly. Stir the mixture again just before serving. For 4.

GLASSWORT *(Salicornia europaea)*

The glasswort prefers saline soil in brackish marshes, along tidal flats far inland, and up and down the east and west coasts of this continent. The plant is annual with upright stems, or lower branches prostrate and branching. Numerous stems grow one to six inches long. The tops remain tender and tasty from spring to late fall and can be eaten raw. Glasswort can be gathered all season long and makes an excellent summer dish.

My introduction to this appealing plant was in New Brunswick where my host invited me to gather a basketful of the plants from the tidal flats. On our return, the greens were simply rinsed off and any wilted and discolored parts discarded. Then they were put into a big pot and lightly boiled without salt for 15 minutes. All the family soon crowded around the pot to help themselves. For the more timid of us, some of the greens were served on a dinner plate, smothered with melted butter. Believe me, I was very much taken with the fresh, exquisite taste of this plant.

A couple of nights later we had the same plant as an hors d'oeuvre, but this time it had been pickled in white vinegar and spices. Here is that recipe.

PICKLED GLASSWORT

1 pound glasswort tips, about 3 inches long	1 cinnamon stick to each glass jar
2 cups white vinegar	1 teaspoon anise seeds
1 cup sugar	1 teaspoon celery seeds
1/2 teaspoon ground cloves	

Wash and clean the glasswort tips and cut into 3-inch lengths. Place in scalded jars with tight-fitting lids. Leave a generous amount of space for the liquid.

Simmer vinegar, sugar, cloves, anise seeds, and celery seeds for 15 minutes. Place one cinnamon stick in each of the jars and pour the liquid over the glasswort. Fill about three-quarters full and cool to room temperature. Then seal and store in a cold place for at least 2 weeks before tasting them — if you can! The longer the pickles stand, the better the result. Pickle as many jars as possible because when you open them, they just don't hang around!

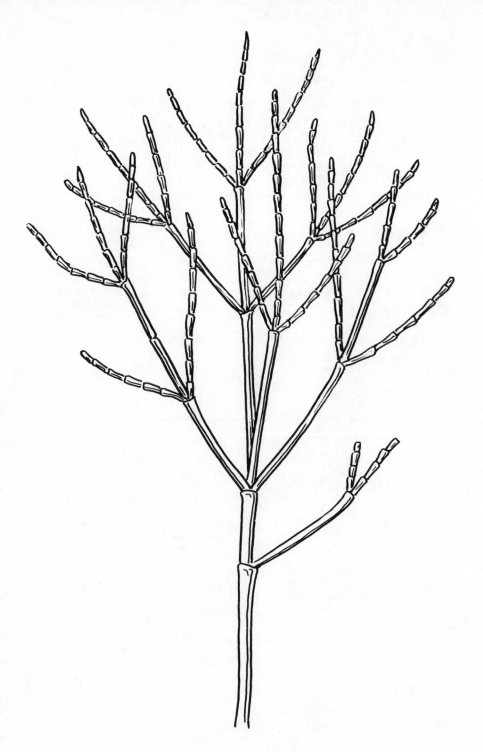

Glasswort

Edible Roots and Tubers 5

INDIAN BREADROOT *(Psoralea esculenta)*

Also called prairie potato or by the Indian name, tip-sin-nah, the Indian breadroot was very important to the North American Indians and highly esteemed by the Sioux. The plant, with its much enlarged root, grows from Manitoba to British Columbia in the north and along the western seaboard to Mexico. The visible part of the plant consists of long hairy stems with yellowish or pale blue flowers.

Indian breadroot should be dug up in midsummer when the leaves are dry and beginning to turn brown. Because it grows in parched prairie soil, it is advisable to take a good spade with you when gathering the roots, as the ground is usually hard. If you delay too long, the plant is not easy to find as the foliage blows away in the strong winds.

The roots have a sweetish, turnip-like taste and can be eaten raw, peeled and roasted, or boiled. Occasionally, the Indians dried them and ground them into flour for cake-baking, or, thinly sliced, they were stored for winter consumption.

Like the Irish, many a settler has kept hunger away from his door with the help of this staple food.

STEWED BREADROOTS

1¹/₂ pounds breadroot	3 tablespoons cream
1 bouillon cube	2 tablespoons butter
1¹/₄ cups water	1 teaspoon sugar
2 egg yolks	¹/₂ teaspoon salt

Clean, peel, and dice the breadroots. In a medium saucepan dissolve the bouillon cube in the water and add the breadroots. Bring to a boil, lower the heat, and simmer until soft. Remove the pan from the heat and set aside.

Blend the egg yolks with the cream. Strain the breadroots from the bouillon in the pan and set aside. Add the egg and cream mixture to this liquid, stirring constantly. Stir over low heat until the sauce thickens, but do not let it boil. Add butter, sugar, salt, and diced breadroots. Good with any meat dish. Serves 4.

ROAST BREADROOTS WITH CHEESE

4 large breadroots	1 teaspoon paprika
1/2 cup margarine	1/2 cup cheese, finely grated
1 teaspoon salt	

Preheat oven to 400°F. Wash and peel the breadroots. With a sharp knife slice them thinly half way through. Melt the margarine in a one-quart casserole, turn the breadroots in it, and sit them in the casserole, sliced side up. Sprinkle with salt and paprika. Roast in the oven for 45 minutes, basting frequently. Then remove the casserole and sprinkle the grated cheese over the breadroots. Lower the heat to 325°F and put it back in the oven for a further 30 minutes, without basting. These are very tasty with any roasted meat.

SWEDISH KROPKAKOR

6 large breadroots	1/4 pound smoked bacon, diced
1 egg	1 bouillon cube
1 cup flour	1 tablespoon salt
1 chopped onion	

Wash and peel the breadroots. Put them in the saucepan on a high heat and bring to the boil. Lower the heat and continue to boil until they are soft. Drain. Mash breadroots with a potato masher and leave to cool.

Mix the mashed breadroots, egg, and flour until it can be easily rolled out to about an inch thick. Cut out rounds with a cookie cutter or a glass. Mix the bacon and onions in a bowl. Place a teaspoon of the bacon and onion mixture in the middle of each circle and close up into a ball.

Half fill a 2-quart saucepan with water, add the bouillon cube, and salt; bring to a boil over high heat. Lower the heat until the water is

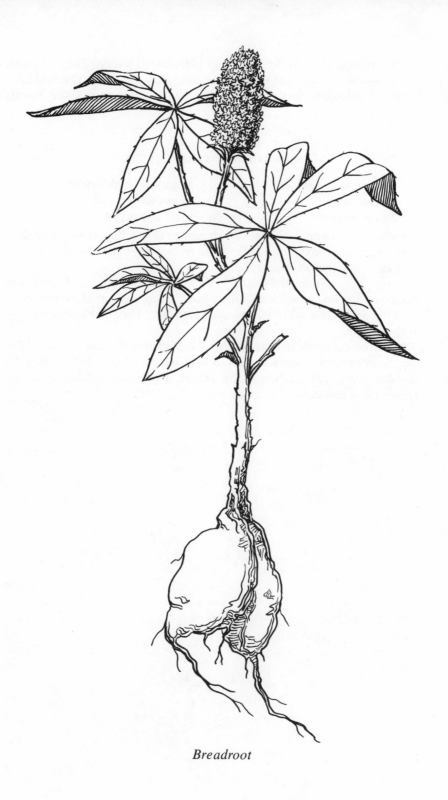

Breadroot

slowly rolling, and add the breadroot balls one at a time. They will sink to the bottom at once and will not rise until they are done. This will take about 35 minutes. Serve them with melted butter or a white sauce. Serves 6.

BREADROOT TEMPTATION

5 medium breadroots	5 smoked frankfurters
2 large onions	2 cups table cream
1/2 cup butter	salt and pepper

Preheat the oven to 375°F. Wash and peel the breadroots and slice fairly thinly. Remove the skin from the frankfurters and also slice thinly. Peel and slice the onions.

Butter a casserole and place half the breadroots in it. Spread the onions on top and cover with a little butter. Lay the frankfurters evenly over the onions and add the remaining breadroot slices. Dot with the rest of the butter.

Place the casserole in the oven for about 10 minutes, then add half the cream and sprinkle with some salt and pepper. Cook for another 10 minutes, then add the remaining cream. Continue cooking until the breadroot is tender — about one hour.

JACK-IN-THE-PULPIT *(Arum triphyllum)*

This plant is sometimes called Indian turnip, but as cheeky young schoolboys, we called it memoryroot. When visited by friends or relatives from the city, we had a favorite trick. We invited the unsuspecting guests to take a hearty bite of the corm. Particularly when fresh, these corms have such an intensely acrid juice that it causes a violent burning sensation of the mucuous membranes and swelling in the mouth — a bite that they never forgot and hence the name "memoryroot." However, this acridity is destroyed by heat or by drying; then the roots are nutritious and good to eat. Perhaps it was my conscience then that made me reluctant to try a dish made from this plant by my Indian guide, but, to my great surprise, the plant tasted much like a turnip!

This erect herb grows to a height of eight to twenty inches in boggy spots in deep, rich woods. The root is a coarsely reticulated, wrinkled corm with a great number of rootlets sprouting from the base of the stalk. The leaves are single or in pairs, ovate, pointed, and free-sectioned. The spadix is club-shaped. The fruit, after the spadix has died, is composed of four to six scarlet berries with seeds.

The plant is found in most parts of Canada and the United States. The roots were highly thought of by the North American Indians and were a part of the daily diet.

WILD APPLE AND JACK-IN-THE-PULPIT ROOT

6 tart wild apples	1 teaspoon salt
6 jack-in-the-pulpit roots	$^1/_2$ teaspoon pepper
$^1/_2$ cup brown sugar	4 link sausages
$^1/_4$ cup butter	

Preheat the oven to 325°F. Wash and peel the apples, remove the cores, and cut in thin slices. Wash and scrape the roots and slice thinly. Butter a small casserole and place a layer of sliced apples in it. Sprinkle with the brown sugar and lay some of the sliced roots on them. Season with salt and pepper. Repeat until the casserole is full. Put the link sausages on top. Leave in a cool place for at least an hour.

Dot the top layer with the rest of the butter and bake for 45 minutes until browned and tender. Check with a toothpick. Serves 4.

JACK-IN-THE-PULPIT PANCAKES

2 cups dried jack-in-the-pulpit roots	$^1/_4$ cup water
	$^1/_4$ cup flour
2 eggs, beaten	$^1/_4$ teaspoon salt

Crush the dried roots; mix with the water and beaten eggs. Add the salt and flour to make a runny batter. Drop by the spoonful on to a hot griddle. Serve with cranberry jelly.

Jack-in-the-Pulpit

JACK-IN-THE-PULPIT ROOTS AND CHIVES

1¹/₄ pounds jack-in-the-pulpit roots
¹/₄ cup margarine
¹/₄ teaspoon hickory salt

pepper
1 tablespoon chives, finely chopped

Wash and peel the roots. Boil until tender (20 to 25 minutes), drain, and cool.

Melt the margarine in a large skillet and add the roots. Season with hickory salt, pepper, and chives. Heat thoroughly, turning the roots gently so as not to break them up. Serve as hot as possible. Serves 4.

CREAMED JACK-IN-THE-PULPIT ROOTS

2 pounds jack-in-the-pulpit roots
2 tablespoons butter
2 tablespoons flour

¹/₂ teaspoon salt
¹/₈ teaspoon pepper
1¹/₂ cups milk

Wash and peel the roots. Cook until tender for 15 to 20 minutes, then drain and keep warm.

Melt the butter in a double boiler, mix in the flour and seasoning, and, still stirring, slowly add the milk. Stir until the sauce is smooth and boiling. Reduce to simmer for about 15 minutes. Add the roots and heat thoroughly for another 5 minutes.

SPRING LAMB STEW WITH JACK-IN-THE-PULPIT ROOTS

2¹/₂ pounds stewing lamb
2 pounds jack-in-the-pulpit roots
4 wild onions

4 wild leeks, finely chopped
1 tablespoon salt
¹/₂ teaspoon pepper
4 cups water

Preheat the oven to 325°F. Cut the lamb into suitable servings. Wash and scrape the roots and slice thinly. Place the meat, roots, onions, and finely chopped leeks layer by layer in a casserole, seasoning each layer with salt and pepper. Pour the water over; cover tightly. Allow to rest in a cool place for 30 minutes. After half an hour, cook the stew in the oven for at least 2¹/₂ hours. Garnish with parsley just before serving. Will serve 6 people.

MARIPOSA LILY *(Calochortus macrocarpus)*

All our native species of lilies are edible but to the Mormons of 1848 they were more than just good to eat. The Mariposa or Sego lily was what stood between them and starvation when their crops were devastated by locusts.

The Mariposa lily grows in Alberta, British Columbia, along the Rocky Mountains, south to Mexico. The small bulbs are extremely sweet and can be either roasted or eaten raw. Many Indian tribes dried them, and pounded them into a flour for porridge or mash. But the bulbs had the added advantage of keeping for long periods without deterioration and so were an excellent winter food for Indians and settlers alike.

This plant grows up to two feet tall with narrow leaves and bright purple flowers with variable dark markings at the base of the petals.

ROASTED MARIPOSA BULBS

If you would like to pleasantly surprise your barbecue guests, serve Mariposa bulbs roasted in traditional Indian fashion.

Dig a hole in the ground about one foot square, line it with flat stones, and build a fire in the pit. When the stones are good and hot, rake out the coals and place a layer of pine needles in the bottom. Lay the bulbs on top and cover with another layer of pine needles. Rake the coals back over the needles and start a small fire on top. After about an hour the bulbs are ready to be taken out and enjoyed.

FRIED MARIPOSA TUBERS IN SOUR CREAM

¹/₂ cup wild onions, finely chopped	4 tablespoons butter
1 pound Mariposa tubers, thinly sliced	¹/₄ cup dry bread crumbs
	¹/₂ cup sour cream

Melt the butter in a heavy, stainless steel skillet over high heat. Add the chopped onions and cook for 5 minutes until they are transparent but not brown. Add the sliced Mariposa tubers and cook for another 5 minutes. Shake the pan from time to time so that the onions and tubers

Mariposa Lily

do not stick. When the tubers are a delicate brown, sprinkle the bread crumbs over them and toss lightly with a spatula.

Beat the sour cream with a wooden spoon or whisk for a minute or two, then stir it into the skillet. Toss lightly until everything is well coated. Serve with meat or fish. Serves 4.

MARIPOSA TUBERS IN CREAM SAUCE

1 pound Mariposa tubers	1 cup milk
2 teaspoons salt	1 cup heavy cream
4 tablespoons butter	$^1/_2$ teaspoon pepper, freshly
4 tablespoons flour	ground

Wash and clean the tubers, removing the outer scales. Cut into small pieces. Place the tubers in a saucepan, tightly covered, over medium heat for about 15 minutes. Drain, chop very finely, and set aside.

In a medium saucepan, melt the butter over medium heat, add the flour, and stir. Add the milk a little at a time, continuing to stir, then the cream. Beating vigorously with a wire whisk, lower the heat, cook until the sauce comes to a boil, and is smooth and thick. Add the remainder of the salt, the pepper, and, finally, the Mariposa tubers. Cook for another 5 minutes until they are heated through. Serve with pork or smoked fish. Six servings.

DILLED MARIPOSA BULBS

20 small Mariposa lily bulbs	$^1/_8$ teaspoon pepper
8 tablespoons margarine	3 tablespoons fresh dill,
1 teaspoon salt	finely chopped

Scrub the bulbs under cold running water to remove any scales. Dry with paper towels. Melt the butter in a heavy 6-quart covered casserole. Add the tubers and sprinkle them with salt. Coat the tubers thoroughly by rolling them in the melted margarine.

To have any success with this dish the cover must fit the casserole tightly; if not, the steam will escape and the tubers will be soggy. It helps to use a double thickness of aluminum foil to cover the casserole first. Then place the lid on top, with the aluminum foil folded down around the rim of the casserole to assure a tight seal.

Cook on low for 30 to 45 minutes, depending on the size of the tubers. Shake the casserole from time to time to prevent the tubers from sticking. When they can be pierced with the tip of a sharp knife, they are done. Place them on a heated serving plate, sprinkle the chopped dill over them, and serve at once. Serves 4.

BISCUIT ROOT *(Peucedanum ambigum)*

In many an early explorer's diary the biscuit root was referred to as the cowas root. The West Coast and west of the Rocky Mountains is its natural habitat, but the plant has been found growing on the Canadian prairies, where it is called *Racine blanc*.

The root is dug up in April or May when the plant is in bloom. When fresh it tastes like parsnip; when it dries out, it becomes brittle and very white, and tastes just like a mild celery. It can be easily pounded into flour. Both the root and the flour keep for several months, but, strangely enough, after bread has been made with it, and the bread is stored for some time, it tastes like stale biscuits. Hence the name — biscuit root.

The Kato Indians dried the roots, then pounded them into flour which they pressed into flat, rectangular cakes. The cakes were about a foot wide, up to three feet long, and about a quarter-inch thick! A hole in the middle meant the cakes could be hung on a pole for storage or made more portable when travelling, and easy to hand for a quick snack. Hungry travellers could simply break off a piece and chew it. For a more sustaining meal, the cakes were pounded into a flour again and mixed with water to make a coarse gruel.

BISCUIT ROOT PANCAKES

2 cups biscuit root flour, coarsely pounded	2 teaspoons salt
1/2 cup water	1/2 teaspoon pepper
2 tablespoons fresh chives, chopped	2 tablespoons butter
	2 tablespoons vegetable oil

Mix the coarsely pounded flour with the water to a smooth paste. Add the chives and spices. Heat the butter and oil in a medium-sized skillet over high heat. The pan must be very hot but not smoking. Use 2 tablespoons of the mixture for each pancake. Fry 3 or 4 at a time, flattening them out with a spatula to about 3 inches in diameter. Fry each batch of pancakes for 3 to 4 minutes on each side, until they are crisp and golden. Serve with whole cranberries.

BISCUIT TUBER CASSEROLE

1 pound biscuit tubers, scrubbed and diced	1 teaspoon salt
¹/₄ cup dry bread crumbs	2 eggs, lightly beaten
¹/₂ cup heavy cream	2 teaspoons margarine
¹/₂ teaspoon nutmeg	2 tablespoons butter

Preheat the oven to 350°F. Place 4 cups of diced biscuit tubers in a 4-quart enameled saucepan. Pour in enough water to just cover the tubers and add the salt. Bring to a boil, then simmer for 15 minutes. Drain the tubers and force them through a sieve with the back of a wooden spoon into a small bowl.

Soak the bread crumbs in the cream for a few minutes. Stir in the nutmeg, salt, and the lightly beaten eggs; add the puréed tubers and mix thoroughly.

Grease a 2-quart casserole or baking dish with 2 tablespoons of margarine and fill with the mixture. Dot with butter and bake uncovered for one hour, or until the top is lightly browned. Serve hot with pork or ham. Serves 4.

BISCUIT ROOT CAKES

8 tablespoons margarine	2 cups biscuit root flour
¹/₄ cup sugar	¹/₄ cup honey

Melt the margarine in a large, heavy skillet over moderate heat and stir in the sugar. Boil for 20 seconds, making sure that the mixture does not burn. Add the coarsely crushed biscuit root flour, stirring occasionally. Cook for 10 minutes, or until the crushed flour is golden brown. Remove from the heat and stir in the honey, making sure that it dissolves completely.

Rinse a muffin tin in cold water and shake out the excess moisture. Firmly pack the bottom and sides of each muffin cup with the biscuit root mixture, dividing it equally. Refrigerate for at least 3 hours. Loosen the cakes from their container by running a knife around the edges and gently sliding them out. Fill with any fruit jelly. Makes 12.

BISCUIT ROOT BALLS

1¹/₂ pounds biscuit root tubers   cornflakes
1 egg   marshmallows
1 teaspoon salt

Wash and scrub the biscuit root tubers. Place in a saucepan, cover with water, and add the salt. Simmer for 20 minutes. Drain the tubers and, using a potato masher, mash them well. Form into small balls with a marshmallow in the centre of each. Roll in cornflake crumbs, and bake in the oven at 350°F until they open. Serve hot with butter and cranberry jelly.

MAN OF THE EARTH OR GINSENG *(Panax quinquefolius)*

This perennial plant grows in fertile, shady woods, its roots often taking the shape of a man. The name, Man of the Earth, is a translation of the Chinese "jin-Chen" which literally means "like a man."

The plant grows to a height of about twelve inches. The stem is straight and the leaves are divided into five sections. Leaflets are stalked, obovate, narrow, serrated, and pointed. The fruit is a cluster of bright red, twin-celled, kidney-shaped, fleshy berries.

It was in 1718 that the Canadian Jesuits first began shipping the roots to China. By the middle of the century they fetched a dollar a pound here but commanded nearly five dollars a pound in China. Fortunately for the survival of the American ginseng, the Chinese lost their taste for the imported product and now its commercial harvesting has almost ground to a halt. The Indians were aware of the plant's nutritional value, and, so the story goes, combined with several other plants, it made a powerful love potion. The Meskwaki Indian women mixed ginseng root with mica, gelatin, and snake meat, believing it would lure a potential mate. And, according to anthropologist Dr. Michael Weiner, the Pawnees concocted a potion of ginseng, wild columbine, cardinal flower, and carrot-leaved parsley for a powerful love-charm.

ROASTED GINSENG

6 medium ginseng roots   1 teaspoon salt
1 tablespoon butter   2 tablespoons dry bread
3 tablespoons margarine,   crumbs
   melted   2 tablespoons grated cheese

Preheat the oven to 425°F. Wash and scrape the roots and drop them in a bowl of cold water. Place the roots one at a time in the bowl of a spoon large enough to hold the root. With a sharp knife, beginning about half an inch from one end, slice through the root at about quarter-inch intervals. The spoon will prevent the knife from slicing all the way through.

Butter a baking dish large enough to hold the roots side by side in one layer, cut side up. Baste the roots with half the margarine, sprinkle with the salt, and bake in the middle of the oven. After 40 minutes top with the bread crumbs, add the remaining margarine, and baste with the juices in the dish. Continue to roast for another 20 minutes. Sprinkle the cheese over the dish and serve hot. Serves 6.

FRIED GINSENG

1¹/₂ pounds medium ginseng roots	¹/₂ cup butter or margarine
	1 teaspoon salt
4 tablespoons flour	¹/₄ teaspoon pepper

Clean and wash the ginseng roots; place them in a 2-quart saucepan, and add cold water to cover. Bring to a boil, lower the heat, and simmer until the skins are soft. Pour off the water and allow the roots to cool. Peel and slice the roots half an inch thick. Mix together the flour, salt, and pepper on a plate. Melt the butter or margarine in a skillet. Coat the slices of ginseng root in the flour mixture and fry until golden brown on each side. Serve with any meat dish. Serves 4.

STEWED GINSENG

1¹/₂ pounds large ginseng roots	2 tablespoons parsley, chopped
2 tablespoons butter	
¹/₂ tablespoon flour	1 teaspoon salt

Scrape and wash the ginseng roots. Cut into french-fry strips. Place in a 2-quart saucepan on the heat and add enough water to cover the ginseng. Bring to a boil and simmer until the strips are soft. In another saucepan, melt the butter and stir in the flour. Gradually add some of the stock from the ginseng roots, stirring constantly until smooth and all the stock is used up.

Put the root strips and the chopped parsley into the sauce and simmer for a few minutes until all is thoroughly hot. A good accompaniment to any meat dish. Serves 4.

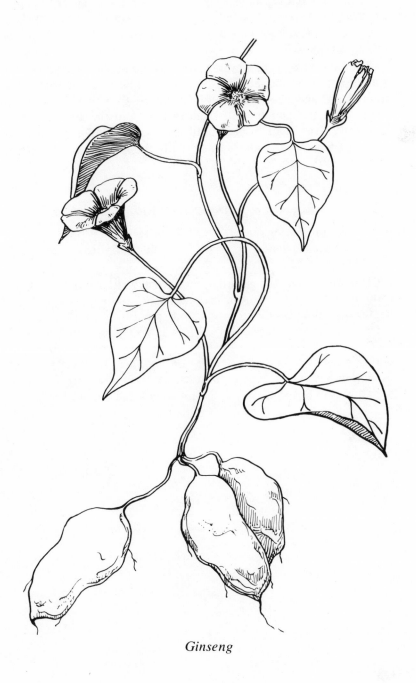

Ginseng

CREAMED GINSENG

6 medium ginseng roots	$1/2$ teaspoon pepper
2 cups sour cream	2 tablespoons chives, finely
$1/4$ cup onion, finely chopped	chopped
1 teaspoon salt	

Clean and scrape the ginseng roots. Simmer them in water until the roots are soft. Remove from the stove, allow to stand for 5 minutes, drain them, and chop into half-inch cubes. Combine the sour cream, onion, salt, and pepper in a large skillet. Add the ginseng roots; stir frequently over medium heat until the cream bubbles and the ginseng roots are heated through. Garnish with chopped chives and serve hot with any fatty meat.

GINSENG CAKES

4 medium ginseng roots	$1/2$ teaspoon pepper
2 tablespoons flour	oil for frying
1 teaspoon salt	

Clean and scrape the ginseng roots, wash well, and pat dry. Grate the roots into a large bowl. Add the salt, flour, and pepper. With a rotary beater or whisk, beat vigorously until smooth.

Heat about 1 tablespoon of oil in a large frying pan. Put in about 3 tablespoons of the ginseng mixture in separate heaps, and flatten them into thin cakes with a spatula. Fry on high heat until crisp and golden brown on both sides. Keep hot in the oven on a serving dish until they are all ready. Serve with whole cranberries and bacon. Serves 4.

GROUNDNUT *(Apios americana* or *tuberosa)*

The groundnut, or Indian potato, is a climbing vine which usually clings to bushes or tree trunks. Leaves are divided into five to seven broad, sharply pointed leaflets. The fragrant flowers grow in short, thick clusters in the leaf axis, not unlike peas, but have a dark maroon or chocolate color. It grows from Nova Scotia to Ontario and southward.

This was one of the plants which, thanks to the Indians who taught them it was edible, helped the Pilgrim Fathers sustain life during that first winter in New England. Ungratefully, however, in 1654 a law was passed which forbade the Indians to dig for the groundnut on "English land." If apprehended, it resulted in a jail sentence. The Indians called the plant Hapniss and this name is used in New Jersey to this day.

The tubers, which resemble potatoes, can be eaten raw or boiled. The groundnut is extremely valuable because it contains up to 18 percent protein by weight.

GROUNDNUT BREAD

10 large groundnut tubers   3 tablespoons butter or
1 teaspoon salt   margarine
1 cup flour

Place the groundnuts in a saucepan, cover with water, and bring to a boil. Lower the heat and simmer until the tubers are well done. Peel the tubers and mash. Cool well so that the mashed groundnuts will not absorb too much of the flour.

Melt the butter in a small pan, add the mashed tubers, the cup of flour, and the salt. Mix well. Take a small amount of the dough and roll out as you would for a pie crust. Make sure that the dough is very thin. Bake on top of a wood stove or on a pancake grill until light brown, turning frequently to prevent scorching.

When golden, wrap in a cloth to keep from drying out.

GROUNDNUT SAUSAGE

¹/₂ pound smoked moose meat   1 teaspoon salt
6 large groundnut tubers   ¹/₂ teaspoon pepper
1 small onion   sausage casings

Wash and scrape the groundnuts, making quite sure that all the skin is removed. Cut the moose meat in small pieces. Peel the onion and slice. Pass the meat, onion, and groundnuts through a meat grinder. (If you don't have one, don't worry — the Indians didn't either. They simply chopped it all into small pieces.) Rinse the casings well. (Your local butcher will probably have them.) Put the meat through the grinder once more, place in a bowl; add the salt and pepper. Mix it all up well, and fill the casings loosely to prevent them from breaking when they boil. Using

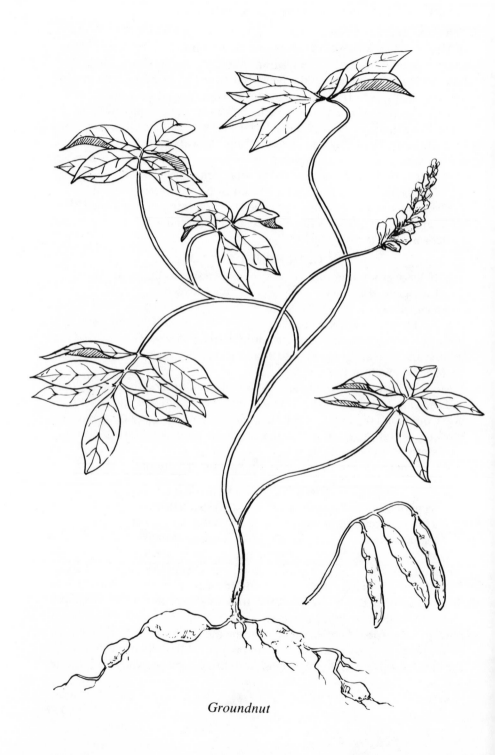

Groundnut

a very sharp fork or a toothpick, puncture the casings in several places. Simmer the sausages in boiling water for at least 45 minutes. Serve with pepper root sauce.

SUMMER VEGETABLE SOUP

8 medium groundnut tubers	1 cup milkweed flowers
4 medium wild carrots	2 teaspoons salt
1 cup dandelion leaves, finely shredded	4 tablespoons butter
	2 cups milk
1 cup common plantain, finely shredded	1 egg yolk
	$1/2$ cup heavy cream

Make sure that all the vegetables are young, fresh, and green. Wash, scrape, and dice the groundnut tubers and wild carrots into quarter-inch pieces. Place all the greens and vegetables in a 2-quart saucepan and cover with cold water. Add the salt and half the butter, and bring to the boil, uncovered, on medium heat. Lower the heat and simmer for 5 minutes until all the greens are tender. Take off the heat and strain the liquid through a fine sieve into a bowl. Set the vegetables and the stock aside in separate bowls.

Melt the remaining 2 tablespoons of butter in the pan over slow heat and, stirring, add the milk and part of the stock, making sure that this does not boil. In a small bowl beat the egg yolk and cream, whisk in a cup of the remaining stock, and add to the milk mixture, stirring well. Add the vegetables to the stock and bring to a simmer, making sure that the soup never boils. Simmer for 10 minutes until the vegetables are heated through. Taste the soup for seasoning, and, if necessary, add salt, pepper, and a little sugar. Pour into a heated soup tureen and serve immediately. Serves 6.

GROUNDNUT DUMPLINGS

4 cups groundnut tubers, grated	2 cups flour
	meat broth or beef bouillon cube
1 teaspoon baking powder	
1 teaspoon salt	

Wash and scrape the groundnut tubers well, then grate them medium coarsely. In a bowl combine the tubers, salt, and flour, and, last of all, add the baking powder. Bring the broth to a boil in a large saucepan. When it boils, roll the dumpling mixture into balls and drop the balls into the broth, a few at a time, so that the broth does not leave the boil. When all the dough is used, lower the heat, cover the pan, and simmer the dumplings for at least an hour. Serves 6.

Hog Peanut

HOG PEANUT *(Amphicarpa bracteata)*

The hog peanut is a native of the territory from Manitoba to Nova Scotia southward, and is usually found in damp woods. It's a delicate, climbing vine with well-formed, pointed, light green leaflets. The plant is quite unique as it has two different kinds of flowers. The flower in the axis of the leaves is lilac-like, droops in clusters, and produces a curved pod with three or four mottled beans, while the pinky-red, petal-less flower at the base of the plant produces a fleshy, single-seeded pod.

In the hog peanut we have another example of a plant that was widely sought and appreciated by the Indians and, later, by the first pioneers. The fruits were eaten in huge amounts by the Indians because of their nutritional value — they are 25 percent protein, the richest source of protein in any wild plant.

The fruits can be eaten raw or boiled. First, the tough, leathery outer shell has to be boiled to get at the beans inside. The Indian practice was to soak the beans in warm water and a small amount of hardwood ashes, and to eat them raw.

The best time of year to gather these fruits of the earth is in the spring or late fall.

BOILED HOG PEANUTS

1 pound bean-sized, shelled, hog peanuts	5 tablespoons butter
3¹/₂ pints water	¹/₂ cup brown sugar
2 teaspoons salt	¹/₄ cup vinegar

Place the hognuts, covered with water, in a 2-quart saucepan on the stove and bring to a boil. Remove from the heat and stand for 5 minutes before draining off the water. Shell the nuts. Pour the 3¹/₂ pints of water into a bowl and add the nuts. Let stand overnight in the water.

Empty the bowl of nuts and water into a saucepan. Add 1 teaspoon of salt, 1 tablespoon of the butter, and bring to a boil. Lower the heat and simmer, covered, until tender. Pour off the water and set aside. Thicken the nuts with the flour, adding vinegar, sugar, 4 tablespoons of butter, and salt. Add some of the reserved cooking water until of the desired consistency. Allow to stand for an hour. Reheat, and serve with bacon or pork. Serves 6.

HOG PEANUT AND BACON CASSEROLE

1 pound hog peanuts	1 cup heavy cream
1/2 pound heavy smoked bacon	1/2 teaspoon salt
3 tablespoons butter	1/4 teaspoon pepper
2 egg yolks	

Place the hog peanuts in a 2-quart saucepan, cover with water, and bring to a boil. Remove and stand for 5 minutes. Drain off the water and shell the nuts.

Preheat the oven to 400°F. Grease a casserole well and spread some of the peanuts on the bottom in an even layer. Cover with sliced bacon. Layer the nuts and bacon alternately and finish with a layer of nuts.

In a small bowl beat the egg yolks with the cream, and add the salt. Pour the mixture over the contents of the casserole, and dot with the butter. Bake in the oven for about 45 minutes or until the nuts are tender. Serve straight from the oven with hot cranberries. Serves 4.

PICKLED HOG PEANUTS

1/2 cup vinegar	1/4 teaspoon black pepper,
1/2 cup water	freshly ground
1/2 cup white sugar	2 cups shelled hog peanuts
1 teaspoon salt	

Place the hog peanuts in a saucepan and cover with water. Bring to a boil, remove from the heat, and set aside for 5 minutes. Drain the water and reserve the nuts.

In a stainless steel or enameled saucepan, combine the vinegar, water, sugar, salt, and pepper. Boil briskly for 3 minutes. Meanwhile, put the hog peanuts in a deep glass, stainless steel, or enameled bowl. Pour the hot marinade over the hog peanuts and let them cool, uncovered, at room temperature.

When cold, cover the bowl with plastic wrap and refrigerate for at least 12 hours, stirring two or three times to keep the nuts moist. Serve with cocktails, Makes 2 cups.

HOG PEANUT SOUP

2 cups hog peanuts, shelled	1 pound lean groundhog
5 cups cold water	meat or
2 wild onions, finely chopped	1 pound piece lean salt pork

Cover the hog peanuts with the water and bring to boil. Remove from the heat and allow to stand for 5 minutes. Drain through sieve, saving the broth and the nuts in separate bowls.

Pour the broth into a 3-quart saucepan and add the meat, the chopped onion, and the clove-studded onion. Bring to a boil over high heat. Lower the heat and simmer for at least 1 hour, partly covered. Add the hog peanuts and simmer for another 30 minutes or until the hog peanuts feel soft. Remove the whole onion and skim off the cloves and small fragments of shell on the surface. Scoop out the meat and cut it into small pieces. Replace the meat and re-heat. Serve in 6 individual soup bowls with a few pieces of meat floating in each bowl.

SWEETFLAG *(Acorus calamus)*

This plant grows in meadows, on pond fringes, and along shorelines, and is easy to recognize. It has sword-like leaves from which the green spadix with its tightly packed florets juts out at an angle from the flat, blade-like stem.

This plant has a long history both as a food and as a medicinal remedy. The Montana Indians boiled the roots and drank the water to induce abortions; the Meskwakis used the boiled root as a salve for burns; and the forest Indians chewed the roots to relieve their colds and toothaches.

It was mostly the floret stalks that were eaten, but small quantities of the root were used to flavor strong-smelling meats like muskrat, bear, and skunk.

SWEETFLAG MARINATED BEAR MEAT

2 pounds bear meat	1 cup vinegar
2 large sweetflag roots	1 cup water
1 cup sugar	2 bay leaves
5 whole peppercorns	2 teaspoons salt

Wash and scrape the sweetflag roots and cut into 1-inch pieces. Combine the vinegar, water, and sugar in a 3-quart enameled or stainless steel saucepan. Boil briskly until all the sugar is dissolved. Add the peppercorns, bay leaves, and salt. Pour it all into a glass container large enough to accommodate the meat as well. Add the piece of meat and the cubed sweetflag roots while the marinade is still hot. Set aside and cool. Refrigerate for at least 12 hours, turning the meat several times.

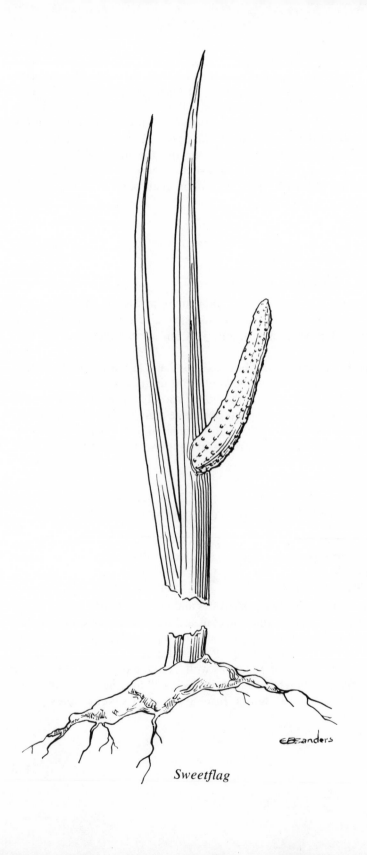

Sweetflag

Preheat the oven to 450°F. Remove the meat from the marinade, pat dry with paper towels, and place it in a roasting pan in the oven for 15 minutes until browned on all sides. Then lower the heat to 400°F and cook until no blood runs out when the meat is pierced with a fork. This will take about 1¹/₂ hours. Remove from the oven and cool on a rack. Slice thinly and serve on toast.

SWEETFLAG SOUP

6 sweetflag florets	4 cups water
¹/₄ cup sweetflag roots, cubed	¹/₂ cups milk
2 tablespoons butter	salt and pepper
2 tablespoons honey	

Scrape and wash the roots and dice small. Wash and clean the florets. Melt the butter and slowly simmer the roots and florets in it for 15 minutes. Add the water and simmer until the roots are cooked. Add the honey and the milk, simmer for another 10 minutes, and the soup is ready to serve. Serves 6.

SMOKED SALMON IN SWEETFLAG SAUCE

1 pound smoked salmon,	2 tablespoons flour
thinly sliced	¹/₂ cup milk
3 cups sweetflag florets	1 hard-cooked egg
¹/₂ cup butter	

Wash and clean the sweetflag florets; pat them dry with paper towels. Remove the flowers from their stalks and set aside. In a 2-quart saucepan melt the butter and add the flour, making a roux. Slowly whisk in the milk until it is a smooth, thick sauce. Lower the heat and simmer for at least 15 minutes while the sauce thickens. Add the sweetflag flowers and simmer until they are heated through.

Spoon the sauce on to a large, heated serving platter. Roll up each slice of salmon, arrange the rolls on the bed of sweetflag sauce, and garnish with chopped egg.

PEPPER-ROOT *(Dentaria diphylla)*

The pepper-root, toothwort, pepper-wort, or crinkleroot is a genus of about thirty species. The leaves appear in pairs almost opposite each other on the stem, and each leaf is divided into three broad leaflets. The flowers range in color from white to pink. The plant can be found from Ontario to the Gaspé, south to Kentucky and Carolina, and as far west as Minnesota.

The Latin name more than likely refers to the tooth-like projections often found on the creeping root-stalks. The Indians enjoyed the root for its watercress-like taste and so do some Europeans, for several species are still cultivated in Europe.

ROLLED VENISON WITH PEPPER-ROOT STUFFING

1¹/₄ pounds venison roast, boneless cut	1 bouillon cube
1¹/₂ cups pepper-root tubers, cut into ¹/₂-inch cubes	1 tablespoon flour
	¹/₂ cup table cream
6 tablespoons butter	1 medium wild carrot
1¹/₄ cups water	1 medium wild onion
	salt and pepper

Cut the meat into four equal portions and pound flat. Season one side with salt and pepper. Wash and clean the pepper-root tubers and cut into half-inch cubes. Melt 2 tablespoons of the butter in a small frying pan over high heat, add the cubed tubers, and simmer in the butter for 5 minutes. Divide the tubers into four equal parts and spread evenly over the pieces of venison. Roll them up and secure with toothpicks. Brown the venison rolls with the wild carrot and onion in the butter left over from browning the tubers. Dissolve the bouillon cube in the water and pour over the meat. Cover tightly and cook gently for an hour, basting from time to time.

Now place the meat in a casserole, keeping it warm in the oven. Strain the stock into a bowl, discarding the carrot and onion. Brown the rest of the butter in the frying pan, scraping the pan to loosen all the bits and pieces. Add the flour and make a roux.

Add the warm stock and the cream and simmer for 10 minutes until the sauce is smooth. Continuing to stir, bring to a boil, then lower the heat and let it thicken. Pour the sauce over the meat in the casserole and keep warm until ready to serve. Serves 4.

Pepper-Root

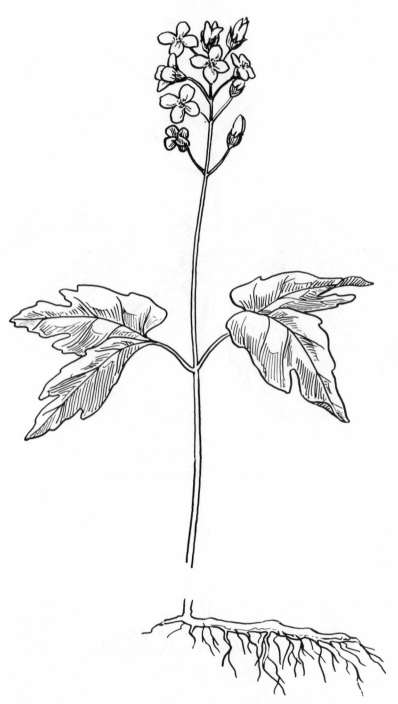

Two-Leaved Toothwort

FRIED PEPPER-ROOT IN SOUR CREAM

4 tablespoons butter	$^1/_4$ cup dry bread crumbs
$^1/_2$ cup onion, finely chopped	$^1/_2$ cup sour cream
1 pound pepper-root, thinly sliced	

In a heavy, large skillet melt the 4 tablespoons of butter over high heat, and, when the butter smells nutty, lower the heat, and add the chopped onions. Cook for 5 minutes until onions are transparent but not brown. Add the pepper-root slices and cook for another 5 minutes. Shake the pan from time to time so that the mixture doesn't stick. When it is a delicate brown, add the bread crumbs, toss the contents of the skillet gently with a wooden spoon, and turn off the heat.

In a small bowl beat the sour cream with a wire whisk for a couple of minutes, then stir it into the skillet. Toss lightly until the onion and pepper-root mixture is well coated with the sour cream.

Serve either cold or warm as an accompaniment to meat or fish. Serves 4.

STEWED PEPPER-ROOTS WITH SOUR CREAM AND DILL

8 medium pepper-root tubers	2 cups milk
2 teaspoons salt	2 tablespoons sour cream
2 tablespoons butter	1 tablespoon watercress
$^1/_2$ cup onion, finely chopped	1 tablespoon dill, finely chopped
2 tablespoons flour	

Wash and scrape the pepper-root tubers well, making sure that all the brown skin is removed. Cut into 1-inch pieces and place them in a bowl. Here you have two choices: either blanch the pepper-roots in boiling water for about 2 minutes, remove and dry; or just place the tubers in the bowl, sprinkle the salt over, toss them around, and let stand for 30 minutes at room temperature. Then drain off all the liquid and pat them dry with paper towels.

In a heavy 10-inch skillet, melt the butter over high heat, lower the heat, and add the onions. Cook until golden brown. Add the flour and cook, stirring constantly, until all is a golden brown color. Watch for burning at this stage and regulate the heat to prevent it. Pour in the milk and bring to a boil, stirring constantly. Reduce the heat and simmer for 2 to 3 minutes until the mixture thickens slightly. Add the pepper-roots and simmer, uncovered, for at least 15 minutes, or until the tubers are tender but not pulpy. Add the sour cream, and, with scissors, snip the watercress finely and add to the mixture. Snip the fresh dill into the pan, too. Simmer over very low heat for 10 minutes and serve in a heated bowl. Serves 6.

STIR-FRIED PEPPER-ROOT TUBERS

1 pound large pepper-root tubers	1 tablespoon soy sauce
	1 teaspoon salt
2 tablespoons sugar	$^1/_4$ teaspoon cayenne pepper
2 tablespoons white vinegar	1 tablespoon peanut oil

Wash and scrape the pepper-root tubers well, making sure that all the brown skin is removed. Cut them into 1-inch cubes and set aside.

Mix together the sugar, vinegar, soy sauce, and cayenne pepper. Place a large, heavy skillet on high heat. Add the peanut oil and swirl the oil around in the skillet for about a minute, then lower the heat to moderate. Add the pepper-root cubes and stir-fry for 5 to 10 minutes, making sure that all the tubers are well coated with the oil. Remove the pan from the heat and stir in the soy-vinegar mixture. Transfer the pepper-root to a platter and cool. Place in the refrigerator and chill thoroughly before serving. Serves 4.

WILD GINGER *(Asarum canadense)*

This plant grows from Quebec to Manitoba, down to Kentucky and Virginia. The single, curious cup-shaped flowers with three red-brown cylix lobes are borne close to the ground and are often hard to see because they are covered by the large, heart-shaped leaves on long, hairy stalks. Along the Pacific coast you will find the western wild ginger *(Asarum caudatum)*.

Wild ginger is highly aromatic and was a favorite ingredient in the forest Indian's stews and soups. The Chippewa Indians were fond of this plant both as a food and, dried, as a remedy for snake bites. This may have been the reason why the plant was often called the Canadian snakeroot.

BAKED RABBIT WITH WILD GINGER STUFFING

1 rabbit	2 tablespoons butter
2 large ginger-roots, quartered	1 teaspoon salt
4 strips heavy smoked bacon	$^1/_2$ teaspoon pepper
2 cups water	1 cup dry bread crumbs
3 cups wild ginger, cubed	

Skin and clean the rabbit. Wash it thoroughly in warm, salted water to remove the blood. Whip the butter in a bowl and add the cubed wild ginger. Stir lightly so that all the cubes are mixed with the butter. Add the salt, pepper, and bread crumbs. Preheat the oven to 400°F. Fill the cavity with the stuffing and sew it up.

Position the rabbit, breast down, on a rack in a baking pan with the legs folded under the body and fastened there with skewers. Arrange the quartered ginger roots around the rabbit. Fasten the strips of bacon over the back of the rabbit with toothpicks to keep the meat from drying out. Place the pan in the preheated oven for 10 minutes, then pour the water over the meat. Continue to bake for about an hour until the meat is tender, basting occasionally. Remove the bacon for the last 10 minutes to allow the rabbit to brown. Serve hot, or cool to room temperature. Slice and serve on hot toast. Serves 6.

BAKED FISH WITH WILD GINGER STUFFING

1 dressed pike (2 to 3 pounds)	2 tablespoons lemon juice
1 cup sliced ginger root	$^1/_2$ cup bread crumbs
2 tablespoons butter	1 tablespoon salt

Wash and scrape the ginger roots and slice thinly. Clean the fish, remove the backbone, but leave head and tail on. Preheat the oven to 450°F.

In a skillet melt the butter over high heat, and, when it smells nutty, lower the heat and add the sliced ginger roots, lemon juice, and bread crumbs. Simmer for 5 minutes and cool. Rub the salt inside the fish. Fill the cavity with the bread crumb and ginger mixture. Lace up the fish with string. Place in a shallow, greased baking dish in preheated oven. Bake for 30 minutes, basting the fish occasionally. Cut away the string before serving with melted butter, using the filling as a condiment. Serves 4.

STEAMED ARCTIC CHAR WITH WILD GINGER STUFFING

1 to 3 pound arctic char	2 tablespoons butter
2 cups diced wild ginger	$^1/_4$ teaspoon pepper
1 tablespoon salt	3 quarts water

Gut the fish, leaving the head and tail on. Wipe clean. Scrape and wash the wild ginger, making sure that all the brown skin is removed. Chop it into half-inch cubes and rinse in cold water. Rub the cavity of the fish with salt, and sprinkle the pepper inside. Stuff the char with the wild ginger cubes, and dot with the butter.

Wrap the fish in aluminum foil, making sure it is completely watertight, or use one of the plastic cooking pouches. Place the wrapped fish in a 4-quart pot and add the water. Bring to a boil, lower the heat, cover the pot, and simmer for 20 minutes, turning the pouch occasionally without puncturing the foil or plastic bag.

Remove the fish and drain the stock into a small sauceboat. Keep warm. Let the fish cool before serving, using the stock for a sauce. Accompany it with a salad.

154

Wild Ginger

VENISON LIVER AND WILD GINGER

1 venison liver	$^1/_4$ teaspoon pepper
1 egg yolk	4 tablespoons bacon fat
4 tablespoons flour	3 cups sliced wild ginger roots
$^1/_2$ teaspoon salt	3 cups water

Slice the liver thinly. Pour boiling water over the slices twice, then pat dry with paper towels. Wash and scrape the wild ginger roots carefully, making sure all the skin is removed. Slice thinly.

Melt the bacon fat in a 10 to 12-inch heavy skillet. Slightly beat the egg yolk in a bowl. Place the flour, salt, and pepper in a brown paper bag and shake thoroughly. Spread the seasoned flour on a dinner plate. Dip the liver in the beaten egg and dredge in the seasoned flour. Sauté the liver in the fat until lightly browned. Add 2 cups of water, cover, and simmer for an hour. Remove the liver, add the sliced wild ginger to the skillet, and sauté until golden brown. Now place the liver back in the skillet and let it simmer slowly with the ginger for another 30 minutes. Serve hot for 4 people.

WILD CARROT *(Daucus carota)*

This plant is known to many of us as Queen Anne's lace or devil's plague. It comes from Asia but became naturalized in America and has spread through Europe. Although we know its origin, we are not sure how or when the plant was introduced to the North American continent. It *was* familiar to the Indians long before any white man set foot on our coast, and is now a common sight in meadows and pastures.

Anthropologist Michael Weiner reports that the Mohegans steeped the blossoms in warm water when they were in full bloom and took the drink as a cure for diabetes. Besides being a potherb, the Indians used the reddish juice as a natural food coloring; the French used it for their liqueurs; and today carrot seed oil is used in perfumes.

The extremely flat clusters of flowers form a lace-like pattern and often develop a single, tiny, deep purple floret in the centre. Old flower clusters curl to form a cup, not unlike a bird's nest. The leaves are finely divided and subdivided. A sure identification of the wild carrot is the stiff, three-forked bracts below the main flower cluster.

HONEY-GLAZED WILD CARROTS

12 medium wild carrots	$^{1}/_{2}$ teaspoon salt
2 tablespoons honey	$^{1}/_{4}$ teaspoon pepper
2 tablespoons butter	1 cup water

Wash and scrape the wild carrots and slice into four, lengthwise, then cut into 2-inch sections. Place the carrots in a saucepan, add the water, salt, and pepper. Bring to a boil and simmer for 10 minutes. Drain off the water. Add the honey and butter, and reheat making sure that the wild carrots are well covered with the mixture.

PICKLED WILD CARROTS

12 small wild carrots	3 cups brown sugar
2 cups vinegar	2 cups water

Choose wild carrots of uniform size. Wash in cold water. Place the carrots in a 2-quart saucepan and cover with water. Bring to a boil, remove from the heat, and let sit for 5 minutes. Take out of the water and rub off the skins. Replace in the water and add the salt. Place over the heat and simmer until they are tender.

Wild Carrot

In another stainless pot combine the vinegar, water, and sugar. Simmer for 5 minutes. Drain the carrots. Pour the vinegar mixture into a clean glass jar and add the carrots. Let stand at room temperature until cool; then seal the jar and store in a cool place for at least 3 days before using.

GLAZED WILD CARROTS

1¹/₂ pounds wild carrots	2 tablespoons honey
1 bouillon cube	4 tablespoons margarine
1 cup water	

Scrape and wash the carrots and cut them in half. In a 2-quart saucepan dissolve the bouillon cube in the water and place the pan over low heat. Add the margarine and honey; stir. Add the carrots and simmer until they are soft and tender. Drain them and set them aside. Reduce the sauce until it is thick. Return the carrots to the sauce and coat them in it by shaking the pan back and forth over low heat. Serve with any kind of meat. Serves 4.

STEWED WILD CARROTS

1¹/₂ pounds wild carrots	3 tablespoons whipping cream
1 bouillon cube	2 tablespoons butter
1¹/₂ cups water	1 teaspoon sugar
2 egg yolks	salt and pepper

Clean, scrape, and dice the wild carrots. Place them in a medium saucepan, cover with water, and bring to a boil. Simmer until they are soft. Drain off the water. Dissolve the bouillon cube in water and return the carrots to the pot. Simmer for another 15 minutes, remove from the fire, and set aside. Mix the egg yolks and cream together and add this mixture to the hot bouillon, stirring constantly. Simmer until the sauce thickens, making sure that it never boils. Add the butter, sugar, salt, and pepper. Stir well and simmer for another 5 minutes. Serve with meat. Serves 4.

INDIAN CUCUMBER ROOT *(Medeola virginiana)*

It is with some misgiving that I even mention this plant because it is indeed rare. Please remember to show a little restraint when gathering this plant because you are destroying a very decorative member of the wild lily family. Nevertheless, I can't leave this delightfully tasty root out of our book.

The Indian cucumber root is unmistakable because of its arrangement of leaves that are fastened halfway up the stem and consist of a whorl of leaves ranging in number from seven to nine. They are elongated and resemble the ribs of an umbrella. At the top of the plant is another whorl of leaves, rarely more than three or four. The yellow flowers appear around those leaves. The edible root, which is very good, is snow white, crisp, and tastes of cucumber. It can be eaten raw or boiled.

PICKLED WILD CUCUMBER TUBERS

6 medium wild cucumber
  tubers
1 cup white vinegar
2 tablespoons sugar
1 teaspoon salt
¹/₄ teaspoon white pepper
2 tablespoons fresh dill,
  chopped

Wash and scrape the fresh tubers. Slice paper thin. Ideally, the slices should be almost translucent. Arrange them in a glass dish. In a small bowl beat together the vinegar, sugar, salt, and pepper. Pour this over the wild cucumbers and sprinkle with the chopped dill. Chill in the refrigerator for at least 2 hours before serving. Serves 4.

INDIAN CUCUMBER TUBERS IN CREAM

3 medium Indian cucumber
  tubers
2 cups whipping cream
1 tablespoon sugar
2 tablespoons vinegar
¹/₂ teaspoon salt
¹/₄ teaspoon white pepper

Wash and scrape the tubers, making sure that all the brown covering is removed. Slice thinly and place them in a glass dish.

In a small mixing bowl, combine the cream, sugar, vinegar, salt, and pepper. Pour over the tubers and chill in the refrigerator for at least 2 hours before serving.

Indian Cucumber

INDIAN CUCUMBER TUBERS IN PARSLEY SAUCE

5 tablespoons olive oil
6 medium Indian cucumber
  tubers
$^1/_2$ cup wild onions, finely
  chopped

2 tablespoons parsley, finely
  chopped
1 teaspoon salt
$1^1/_4$ teaspoon black pepper
$1^1/_2$ cups boiling water

Wash and scrape the tubers; slice into half-inch rounds. In a 10-inch heavy skillet, heat the olive oil on high until a light haze forms above it. Add the cucumber tubers. Turning frequently with a spatula, cook for 10 minutes until they are golden brown all over.

Scatter the onions, parsley, salt, and pepper on top of the tubers and pour in the boiling water. Just shake the pan back and forth for a couple of minutes to distribute the water evenly.

Cover the skillet tightly and simmer over low heat for about 20 minutes, or until the tubers are tender. Shake the skillet again occasionally to prevent the tubers from sticking to the pan. Using a slotted spoon, transfer the tubers to a heated platter and pour some of the cooking liquid over them. Serve the remaining juice separately in a sauceboat. Serves 4.

Wild Plants for Drinks and Spices

6

BLACK BIRCH (*Betula lenta*)

The black birch is common in the eastern part of North America. It is one of nearly forty species of the birch family. Also called mountain mahogany or sweet birch, the black birch is often mistaken for a member of the cherry family.

The bark is reddish brown or almost black — much like the cherry. If in doubt, crush or cut one of the twigs — it will smell of wintergreen. Before oil of wintergreen was manufactured synthetically, it was made from the bark or twigs of the black birch. However, before you go into the business of producing oil of wintergreen, you will need a copper whiskey still.)

Historically, Huron Indians often used the bark or the young twigs both as a stimulant tea and as a food seasoning, as observed by the French explorer, Samuel de Champlain in 1615, during his stay with the Hurons. He found that the women often used black birch bark to improve the taste of their food, which indeed it did.

BLACK BIRCH TEA

Cut a strip of bark from a young tree, or use twigs cut into small pieces. Immerse in water and bring to a boil. Remove from the heat and cool on the side of the stove, letting the mixture stand and brew for at least 30 minutes. Reheat, strain, and serve as a stimulating tea.

Black Birch

BLACK BIRCH MEAT SPICE

Put a small handful of twigs or some bark in a piece of cloth and tie it securely. When boiling meat, add the spice-bag. It will improve the flavor.

SASSAFRAS *(Sassafras albidum)*

Sassafras, the tree with the funny looking leaves, grows from Maine to Ontario and south to Florida and Texas. It is a native of North America. In the northern part of its habitat, sassafras appears as a shrub; but in the southern United States it can reach a height of a hundred feet.

Most Indian tribes in eastern North America utilized this plant for one ailment or another, and, when the Spaniards conquered Florida in 1538, they mistook its scent for cinnamon. They took some bark to Spain, where it soon gained a reputation as a medicine, rather than a spice. Soon it became one of the most common remedies for pain and a score of diseases, and an important export from North America to England.

Sassafras can be identified by its leaves — alternate, simple, oval in outline, long, smooth, and bright green. Often they are two to three-lobed, three to four inches long, and slightly hairy on the underside.

The bark on young stems is thin and reddish brown; the twigs are a shiny, bright green. The dark blue fruit ripens in the fall — oval and berry-like, it is about half an inch long and is borne on a stout, red, fleshy, club-shaped stalk.

SASSAFRAS TEA

Early in the spring, dig up sassafras roots and wash them. Remove the bark by scraping; let it dry in the sun. When dry, crush it and store it in a tight container. To make tea, simply pour some crushed bark into a teapot, pour boiling water over it and steep for 5 to 10 minutes. The tea is said to be good for treating high blood pressure and for inducing perspiration to relieve a cold.

SASSAFRAS WINE

Late in the fall just before the berries drop, collect them. Crush, and place in a fermentation vessel the following:

2 pounds sassafras berries	2 Campden tablets
15 ounces raisins	2 teaspoons yeast nutrient
5 pounds sugar	2 gallons water
2 tablespoons citric acid	1 package wine yeast

Mix all the ingredients (except wine yeast and water) in a primary fermentation vessel. (We use a plastic garbage can with a lid.) Boil the water and pour it over the mixture. Mix well to make sure the sugar has dissolved. Cover. Let stand overnight at a temperature of between 65°F and 70°F.

Next morning, sprinkle the yeast over the surface, and let stand for 24 hours. Ferment in primary fermentation vessel for 6 or 7 days, stirring twice a day. On the fifth day, add a cup of sugar solution (2 parts sugar to 1 part water). Let stand for 2 days, then add another cup of sugar solution. Let stand for 2 more days, then strain the ferment through a fine sieve lined with a double layer of cheesecloth. Allow to stand overnight.

The next day, siphon the liquid into gallon jugs and put fermentation locks (locks that allow fermenting gas to escape) on the jugs. Leave for 3 weeks and then draw off into clean gallon jugs. Let stand for 3 months, draw off again into clean gallon jugs, and leave until the wine is clear and stable.

Add 3 stabilizer tablets per gallon and rack into clean wine bottles.

(The early Pennsylvania Germans used sassafras wine not only as a table wine but also as a cold remedy.)

Sassafras

Spicebush

SPICEBUSH *(Lindera benzoin)*

The spicebush is an aromatic shrub, about six to eight feet tall, inhabiting low, marshy spots along the banks of streams from Ontario to Florida. The leaves are oblong-ovate, pinnately veined, and pale underneath.

Flowers appear in umbel-like clusters of four to six, honey yellow in color, with four deciduous scales surrounding the flowers. The flowers appear before the leaves, in March or April.

The spicebush was well known to the Indians of early times; later, to the settlers who used the dried berries and dried buds as a substitute for allspice.

SPICEBUSH TEA

Collect spicebush leaves and place them in a pot. Bring to a boil. Remove from the heat and cool for at least 30 minutes. Re-boil and serve as ordinary tea.

SPICEBUSH SPICE

Collect the berries in late fall; shred them on a sheet to dry in the sun for 3 to 4 days. Put berries in a cool, dry place for a couple of weeks, then crush them. Store in airtight bottles, and use the berries as a substitute for allspice.

LABRADOR TEA *(Ledum groenlandicum)*

Labrador tea, or, as it is often called, Greenland tea, is found across Canada in bogs and swamps. It is a low-growing bush with alternate entire leaves, clothed underneath in a rust-colored wool. It blooms with a handsome white flower in June or early July. The narrow leaves are highly fragrant when crushed. They were used by the early settlers as a substitute for ordinary tea. The leaves have narcotic properties.

During his arctic expedition of 1819-1822, the explorer, Sir John Franklin, used the leaves of Labrador tea's arctic cousin, the *Ledum decumbens* (a dwarfed linear arctic species).

In the early days, some Indian tribes extracted oil from the leaves for tanning leather or skins.

LABRADOR TEA

Place a handful of leaves in a pot of boiling water; simmer for a few minutes; remove from the heat. When cool, heat again to desired temperature. Stir, adding sugar, or, even better, a teaspoon of honey.

TO PREPARE LEAVES FOR WINTER

Pick Labrador tea leaves while the plant is flowering. Spread them on a shallow pan and dry in the oven on low heat. When dry, crush the leaves and store in an airtight container. To make tea, put 2 to 3 tablespoons of crumbled leaves into a preheated pot, pour boiling water over, and steep for five minutes before serving.

The taste is not unlike Oriental tea, and it has a high Vitamin C content.

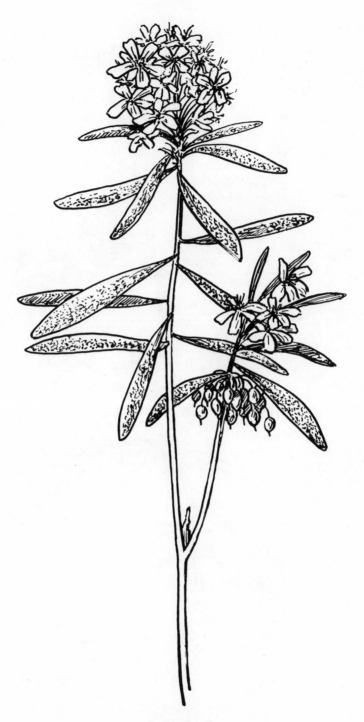

Labrador Tea

Chicory

CHICORY *(Cichorium intybus)*

How often have you admired these clear blue flowers in farmers' fields or along the roadside? Beautiful and abundant, many people mistake chicory flowers for cornflowers.

The ancient Egyptians and Arabians discovered chicory's edible properties — the roots were used to make a drink or a potherb, or they were dried and ground into flour for bread. The bleached leaves were eaten in salads.

In France, roots were dug up, packed in sand, and stored in a dark cellar. All during the winter the roots pushed up shoots which provided a delicate ingredient in a salad.

Chicory's main use, however, has always been as a substitute for coffee — and even today most brands actually have a small amount of chicory in them. Chicory gives coffee a richness and a depth of color, without destroying the true coffee flavor.

Chicory is a perennial plant. It grows to a height of two to four feet. The root is deep and branching, surcharged with a milky juice. The stem has bristly hair with rigid branches; leaves are alternate with a rosette at the base of the plant. Flowers are a clear blue in the early morning and on cloudy days, but they fade and wither in bright sunshine.

CHICORY SALAD

In the early spring and summer, when the first rosette leaves appear, cut them off close to the crown. Wash and clean them, place in a sieve and dip briefly into boiling water. Lift them out and let the water drain away. Tear the leaves into small pieces, cover, and chill until serving time.

The traditional dressing of the early Quebec settlers for this salad was buttermilk dressing. The recipe is given below.

Buttermilk Dressing

2 tablespoons bacon fat	1 cup buttermilk
2 tablespoons flour	1 tablespoon vinegar
2 tablespoons sugar	1 tablespoon grated onion
1 teaspoon dry mustard	1 teaspoon salt

Melt the bacon fat in the top of a double boiler; stir in flour, sugar, and dry mustard. With a wooden spoon, work the roux until smooth. Gradually add the buttermilk, stirring constantly. Cook and stir until thickened and smooth; add salt. Remove from the heat and stir in the vinegar and grated onion. Chill thoroughly before serving.

CHICORY COFFEE SUBSTITUTE

Dig up the roots, clean them free of earth, and dry them in the sun for 4 or 5 days. Then, slice them into thin slices and roast in a 250°F oven for 2 to 3 hours. Grind in the coffee mill and use as ordinary coffee.

GOLDENROD *(Solidago canadensis)*

The goldenrod is a native of North America. Many varieties grow all over this continent—there are about 125 species. In late summer and fall the goldenrod's brilliant yellow flowers can easily be spotted blooming in fields and roadsides.

It is a perennial, with simple undivided leaves bearing many small, spiky flower heads.

Indian tribes chewed goldenrod flowers as a sore throat remedy. The early settlers used both leaves and flowers as a tea substitute.

GOLDENROD TEA

Separate the flowers from the stem, and place in a pot of boiling water. Remove from the heat and steep until cold. Reheat, bring to boil, and strain through a sieve. Serve with honey as a sweetener.

If you want to drink this wonderful tea all year round, pick the leaves and flowers in late summer. Spread them in a shallow pan and dry in a low oven until the leaves crumble easily. When completely dry, store in an airtight container.

To make tea, put a couple of tablespoons of dried flowers and leaves in a preheated teapot. Pour boiling water over, and steep for about ten minutes.

174

Goldenrod

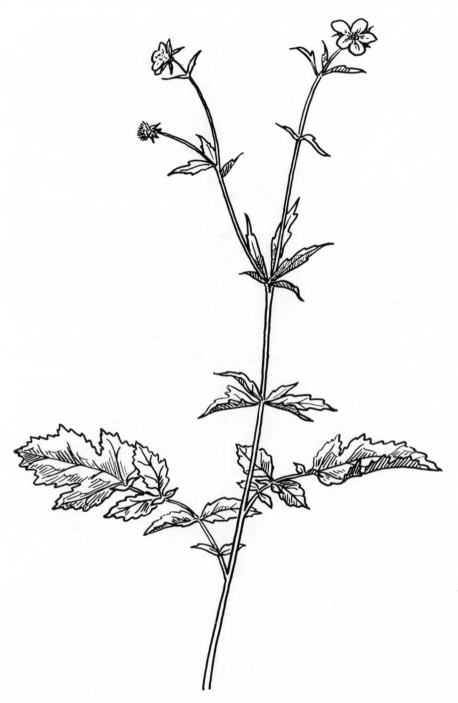

Water Avens

WATER AVENS *(Geum rivale)*

This beautiful perennial with hibiscus-like flowers inhabits bogs and water meadows. It grows from the Canadian Maritime Provinces and Pennsylvania, westward to Wisconsin, and northward.

Water Avens has a creeping root with many rootlets. It has two kinds of leaves—one from the roots on long, deeply grooved peticles, lyrate and irregularly pinnate and another from the stem, more or less lyrate below and three-lobed above, ovate and incised.

Water Avens was also known as Indian Chocolate by the early settlers, and, because of its delicious taste and medicinal properties, may have been one of our earliest sugar-coated medicines.

In the late 1800s, the Thompson Indians of British Columbia used a strong, dark decoction of Water Avens to successfully combat a small-pox epidemic. For the early settlers, the same drink was a standard home remedy to combat dysentry, diarrhea, and stomach upsets.

WATER AVENS CHOCOLATE SUBSTITUTE

Gather roots in the fall or early spring (when they have a sweeter taste). Dry them for a few days in the sun, then slice into 1-inch pieces and store in a cool, dry place. To use, put the desired number of pieces in cold water and bring to a boil. Let stand for 10 to 15 minutes; reheat and serve with cream and sugar.

Index to Illustrations

Index to Plants

182

Index to Recipes